10 Business Commandments for Entrepreneurs: A Blueprint for Building Your Legacy

"I've been in this game for years, it made me an animal, it's rules to this shit, I wrote me a manual"- Notorious B.I.G.

Rules can be a great thing or bad thing; they can enhance your goals or restrict your growth. In both life and business, we encounter unspoken codes that determine who rise and who falls. Biggie Smalls' "10 Crack Commandments" was more than a song; it was a survival guide, a set of essential principles to navigate a high-stakes world. These ten rules became a handbook for survival, dealing with risk, loyalty, ambition, and strategy — all skills transferable to the realm of business.

This book is not about glorifying a lifestyle; it's about recognizing the universal truths that Biggie so astutely distilled into a set of rules. Business and street hustling may seem worlds apart, but both demand grit, calculated risk-taking, and resilience. This isn't your typical business manual, filled with buzzwords and sanitized advice. Instead, it's a raw look at what it takes to succeed by drawing on unconventional wisdom. Every industry has its hidden codes and silent rules and knowing how to play within and around them can mean the difference between success and failure.

In today's ever-evolving business landscape, entrepreneurs are increasingly faced with challenges that can't be solved by textbook answers. There is no one-size-fits-all approach, but rather a set of skills that allow you to navigate the shifting landscape. This book takes Biggie's blueprint and reframes it as a survival manual for the business world. Here, each commandment is reimagined as a principle for entrepreneurship, strategy, and leadership, offering valuable lessons that can help you thrive, whether you're launching a startup, managing a team, or planning long-term growth.

Why These Commandments Matter in Business

We live in a world where a savvy business mindset can mean the difference between growing wealth and squandering potential. The corporate arena and the streets share more similarities than one might think. Whether in an office building or on the streets of Brooklyn, competition is fierce, resources are limited, and loyalty is scarce. Those who succeed are often the ones who understand not only the rules but also the risks, and who have the courage to make tough calls.

Biggie's commandments offer a framework for managing relationships, handling resources, and making strategic moves — all skills that are equally valuable in business. These commandments serve as reminders of the importance of confidentiality, self-discipline, and balancing ambition with caution. They highlight the importance of knowing when to keep your plans close, understanding the value of leverage, and ensuring you aren't weighed down by unnecessary burdens. In business, as in life, the hustler's code teaches us that survival isn't just about winning; it's about staying in the game long enough to change it.

Who This Book Is For

This book is designed for entrepreneurs, business leaders, and anyone who sees the value in blending strategy with street smarts. It's for those who are willing to think outside the box, to take calculated risks, and to learn from unconventional sources. Whether you're starting your first venture, managing a team, or building your legacy, these principles can offer guidance to navigate the journey. The

"10 Business Commandments" present a path forward that is accessible to anyone with the ambition to grow, evolve, and make a lasting impact.

Each chapter will break down one of Biggie's commandments, reinterpreting it through a business lens. You'll find insights into the value of discretion, the power of relationships, the importance of financial discipline, and the necessity of work-life boundaries. Through real-life examples, actionable steps, and reflections, this book gives you tools to adapt Biggie's rules into strategies for success. This approach keeps the book practical and grounded, giving you a roadmap to navigate the highs and lows of building something meaningful.

A Blueprint for Resilience

The "10 Business Commandments" aren't just a list of rules; they're a blueprint for resilience. In a world where the rules are constantly changing, understanding core principles can anchor you amid uncertainty. Business isn't just about profitability; it's about the grit required to bounce back from setbacks, the foresight to know when to pivot, and the determination to see your vision come to life. By translating Biggie's street-inspired wisdom into the language of business, this book offers a fresh perspective on what it takes to succeed, no matter the odds.

In the end, success is about more than just winning; it's about survival, influence, and leaving a legacy. This book is here to remind you that the hustle, in all its forms, is an art. By following these commandments, you're not just following rules; you're writing your own manual — one that, like Biggie's, can guide you through the toughest times and position you to come out on top. Hustling is more than just a word or a concept — it's a mindset, a skill, and a way of navigating through obstacles with resilience, creativity, and adaptability. In the business world, the ability to hustle means having the drive to find opportunities where others see none, to persist through setbacks, and to turn limited resources into valuable assets. This isn't just about working hard; it's about working smart, being strategic, and, like a true hustler, knowing when to make a move and when to hold back. Whether you're an entrepreneur launching a new product or a professional looking to rise in a corporate environment, mastering the art of hustling can be the game-changer that sets you apart.

Resilience and Adaptability: Hustlers are experts in resilience. They understand that failure is not the end; it's a lesson and a stepping stone. In business, resilience is what allows an individual or company to bounce back from setbacks and adapt to changing conditions. Think of Netflix, which started as a DVD rental company and pivoted to streaming before it was mainstream. Their success didn't come from following industry norms but from anticipating the future, adapting quickly, and refusing to let initial setbacks determine their fate. Hustling requires a "never stay down" attitude, and in business, this translates to the ability to pivot, learn from challenges, and stay ahead of the curve.

Resourcefulness and Creativity: Hustling often involves making something out of nothing. When resources are limited, creative solutions are essential. In business, this skill is especially valuable for startups or small companies with tight budgets. Take Airbnb, for example. Founded by two designers who couldn't afford rent, Airbnb started by renting out air mattresses in their apartment and using a borrowed camera to make their space more appealing. With minimal resources, they created an experience, a brand, and eventually a multi-billion-dollar company. Resourcefulness — finding unique ways to solve problems, connect with customers, and grow a business — is central to the hustler's skill set.

Strategic Networking and Relationship Building: True hustlers know that relationships are currency. In business, the ability to build genuine connections with others can open doors, create partnerships, and lead to long-term success. Strategic networking isn't about handing out business cards but about fostering relationships that are mutually beneficial. This theme is evident in the story of Jay-Z, who leveraged partnerships to grow his business ventures and brand. From music to fashion to sports management, Jay-Z's rise is a testament to the power of building relationships. By forming alliances, hustlers gain access to new resources, markets, and opportunities.

Before we dive into specific examples, it's important to understand that the principles of hustling aren't exclusive to one type of person or industry. Hustling as a business skill cuts across backgrounds, company sizes, and industries. Whether you're a solo entrepreneur or leading a global team, the ability to hustle can be your most powerful asset. Hustling is about leveraging what you have, seeking what you need, and pushing boundaries to turn challenges into opportunities. Two entrepreneurs who embody this hustle-driven approach are Sara Blakely and Howard Schultz. Though they come from different industries — fashion and coffee — both used the hustler's mindset to overcome obstacles, break into competitive markets, and redefine their fields. Their stories illustrate the power of resilience, creativity, and drive in transforming ideas into successful, lasting ventures. Let's take a closer look at how each of them hustled their way to the top, turning initial challenges into monumental successes.

Sara Blakely, the founder of Spanx, is a perfect example of a business hustler. When she had the idea of footless pantyhose, she didn't have formal training in fashion or product design. Instead, she taught herself the fundamentals, navigated the manufacturing world by cold-calling factories, and hustled her way into retail stores. She even finessed her way into meetings with high-level executives by showing up unannounced. Blakely's story highlight's key themes of hustling: resourcefulness, adaptability, and relentless determination.

Another compelling example of hustling as a business skill is Howard Schultz, the former CEO of Starbucks. Schultz grew up in a low-income family in Brooklyn, facing financial hardships that fueled his drive to succeed. His journey to build Starbucks into a global coffee empire showcases the power of hustle, resilience, and vision.

When Schultz first joined Starbucks, it was a small company focused on selling coffee beans, not beverages. Inspired by a trip to Italy, where coffee shops were integral parts of the community, Schultz saw an opportunity to turn Starbucks into a place for social connection through coffee. However, when he presented this idea to the owners, they rejected it. Undeterred, Schultz decided to strike out on his own, eventually raising enough capital to open his own coffeehouse, "Il Giornale." This venture became a success, and a few years later, Schultz was able to buy Starbucks and implement his vision of creating a "third place" where people could gather.

Schultz's journey exemplifies the hustle-driven mindset: he identified an opportunity that others overlooked, persisted through setbacks, and creatively secured the resources he needed. His determination transformed Starbucks from a niche coffee retailer into a global lifestyle brand. By refusing to settle for the status quo and staying focused on his vision, Schultz demonstrated how hustling can lead to groundbreaking success in business.

How Hustling Translates to Business Success

Turning Failure into Opportunity: The ability to see failure as a source of growth rather than defeat is essential. Hustlers know that every setback brings valuable information that can fuel future success. Businesses that operate with this mindset are constantly learning and evolving, which allows them to adapt to changing market conditions and customer demands. This is a core advantage of hustle: instead of fearing failure, hustlers embrace it and use it as fuel.

Recognizing Opportunity Where Others Don't: Hustling trains you to think outside the box, to see what others overlook, and to capitalize on these overlooked opportunities. In business, this means spotting trends early, understanding where the market is headed, and finding unique ways to meet demands. Nike, for instance, started by selling Japanese running shoes in the U.S., capitalizing on the demand for affordable athletic footwear. Founder Phil Knight saw potential where others didn't, turning a simple idea into a global empire.

The Power of Perseverance and Grit: Hustlers understand that grit is just as important as talent. Business leaders who persevere through difficulty can stay the course and achieve their long-term goals. In an environment that values quick wins, hustlers are the ones willing to play the long game. By sticking to a vision, even when the payoff isn't immediate, hustlers secure a foothold in competitive markets. Amazon founder Jeff Bezos is a prime example; he built Amazon slowly over the years, reinvesting profits and patiently expanding until it became one of the most powerful companies globally.

Why Hustling Is Needed More Than Ever

In today's fast-paced, ever-changing business environment, the ability to hustle has become indispensable. Technology, market demands, and customer expectations shift quickly, and those who are agile, adaptable, and resilient will be the ones who succeed. Business leaders can no longer afford to stick rigidly to one model or plan. They need to think creatively, adjust quickly, and be ready to take calculated risks. Hustling prepares leaders to do just that.

By studying these examples and understanding the core themes of hustle — resilience, resourcefulness, adaptability, and strategic networking — you can cultivate the mindset needed to thrive. Hustling isn't just about surviving; it's about finding ways to innovate, evolve, and create lasting impact. This book will show you how to apply the hustler's mindset to business, turning challenges into opportunities and limitations into strengths. Like Biggie, you'll be able to navigate the complexities of the game, rising above obstacles to succeed against all odds. Hustling and entrepreneurship are two sides of the same coin. At its core, entrepreneurship is about taking an idea and turning it into a reality, often with limited resources, high risks, and no guaranteed roadmap. It requires the same grit, resourcefulness, and adaptability that define a true hustler. Both hustlers and entrepreneurs are constantly seeking opportunities, driven by the belief that they can make something extraordinary out of seemingly nothing. They know that success isn't about having it all figured out from the start; it's about persevering, learning, and adapting as they go.

To hustle is to think and act like an entrepreneur: spotting possibilities, making quick decisions, and pushing past the boundary's others may see as obstacles. Just as Biggie's commandments served as a street-savvy survival manual, these principles serve as a guide for anyone who wants to create something lasting in the world of business. By combining the hustler's relentless drive with the entrepreneurial spirit, this book aims to empower you to face challenges, find opportunities, and build success on your terms.

Entrepreneurship may be a path filled with uncertainty, but those with the hustler's mindset don't just survive it; they thrive within it. This book will show you how to apply this mindset to create, grow, and succeed in business, turning obstacles into stepping stones and dreams into achievements. Because in the end, whether in the streets or the boardroom, the hustle is all about making your mark and leaving a legacy.

Every hustler knows that there's a code to this — rules that guide the moves, the grind, the resilience. In the streets, those rules were survival. In business, they're strategy. This isn't about bending to limitations; it's about staying focused, moving smart, and building something that lasts. Biggie's commandments might have been laid down with a different game in mind, but the wisdom holds strong in the boardroom, on sales calls, and in every corner where business gets done.

Let's take it commandment by commandment and translate this wisdom from street-level survival to entrepreneurial success. This is more than a guide; it's a way of moving, a mindset. Stick to this blueprint, and you'll see how every principle can empower your growth, sharpen your strategy, and keep you on track, no matter what challenges the business world throws at you.

Commandment 1: Keep Financials Confidential

In the world of business, just like in the hustle, not everyone needs to know what you're holding. Sharing too much can make you vulnerable — it invites judgment, envy, and sometimes even sabotage. It's simple: stay in control by keeping your finances close. When people are left guessing, you maintain the power, and you move on your terms.

Commandment 2: Guard Your Strategy

A hustler knows the importance of a silent move. When you show your hand too soon, you lose your advantage, and someone else might play your moves before you. Business is no different. Guard your strategy, keep it tight, and reveal it only when you're ready to go all-in. Whether you're launching a product, planning an expansion, or making a deal, secrecy is your edge.

Commandment 3: Trust but Verify

Every entrepreneur knows that partnerships and connections are crucial, but blind trust. That's dangerous. Hustling taught us early on that loyalty is earned and people can switch up when you least expect it. So, yes, build relationships — but make sure you're vetting those who get close to your plans. Check credentials, verify promises, and protect your vision. Remember, trust can be an asset, but only when it's guarded with caution.

Commandment 4: Separate Personal from Professional

Hustlers know how easy it is to let business get personal. But in both business and the streets, balance keeps you steady. Keep your business money out of your personal spending, and don't let your home struggles spill into work. Boundaries let you make clear, focused decisions. They let you be strategic, not reactive. In the end, it's this discipline that separates thriving entrepreneurs from those who burn out.

Commandment 5: Keep Home and Work Separate

Where you rest should be where you find peace. Mixing work into your home life too much can mean you're never truly off. A hustler knows the value of keeping these worlds distinct — so when it's time to grind, you're all in, and when it's time to rest, you're recharged. Keep your home a sanctuary, and your mind will stay sharp for the challenges in business.

Commandment 6: Limit Reliance on Credit

Hustling and business both teach that debt is a slippery slope. Once you rely on it, it starts owning you. Use credit carefully, if at all, and avoid taking on more than you can pay off. Build from what you have and grow based on your own resources. That way, you're answering to your vision, not to lenders, and every dollar in your pocket stays under your control.

Commandment 7: Evaluate Family Involvement

Mixing family and business sounds ideal until it doesn't. The reality is, family ties can complicate business goals, adding stress and expectations that can hold you back. Hustlers understand that family and work are two different worlds, and each should be respected. If family is involved, define roles, and set boundaries. Business is business, and it needs to be treated with the same focus, no matter who's involved.

Commandment 8: Reduce Operational Burdens

In both hustling and business, moving light makes you quick on your feet. Don't weigh your company down with excess overhead or unnecessary expenses. Lean operations mean you can adapt faster, move with the market, and stay profitable without a ton of baggage. When you keep things lean, you're always ready for the next opportunity, and the next challenge doesn't feel like a mountain.

Commandment 9: Stay Focused on Revenue Drivers

Every hustler knows the importance of the main hustle over the side distractions. Business can be full of shiny things that look like success but drain time, money, and focus. Stay locked in on what brings in the cash, what builds value, and what moves the needle. In a world full of noise, keep your eyes on the prize.

Commandment 10: Know Your Market Demand

A hustler doesn't waste time on what people don't want to buy. Business is the same — every move needs to be backed by real demand. Know your market, know your customers, and make sure your offerings are aligned with their needs. It's not about throwing out ideas and hoping something sticks; it's about being so in tune with your audience that you're providing exactly what they need, right when they need it.

The game of business isn't for the faint-hearted. It's about moving smart, staying sharp, and sticking to principles that keep you grounded no matter how high you rise. This blueprint — these 10 Business Commandments — are here to set the foundation, to give you a playbook that translates Biggie's wisdom into business moves that work. But knowing the code is just the beginning; it's how you apply it that matters. Each commandment isn't just a rule to follow but a mindset to live by.

In the chapters that follow, we'll dive deep into each commandment, exploring not just the why but the how. We'll look at real-life stories from entrepreneurs, hustlers, and visionaries who have made these principles their own and succeeded because of it. It's about taking the lessons from the streets and applying them to the boardroom, the startup grind, and every corner where business gets done.

So, let's start at the beginning, where it all begins: the power of keeping your financials confidential. Because if there's one thing Biggie knew, it's that not everyone needs to know your business — and the smartest moves often happen behind closed doors. Turn the page, and let's break down Commandment One.

Chapter 1: Keep Financials Confidential

"Never let no one know how much dough you hold." — *Notorious B.I.G.*

The first commandment is as simple as it is powerful: keep your financials close. In business, money isn't just a resource; it's a signal. How you handle it, talk about it, and protect it can make or break your position. Biggie understood this at street level — when everyone knows what you're holding, you lose control, you're open to envy, judgment, and even sabotage. And in business, the rules are just as real.

In this chapter, we're diving into what it means to keep your financials confidential, why it matters for business survival, and how staying tight-lipped about your money can keep you secure, agile, and respected. This isn't about secrecy for secrecy's sake; it's about setting the stage for long-term success. We'll explore how this mindset helps you protect your assets, build credibility, and manage perceptions. Real-life examples from entrepreneurs who have mastered this commandment will show how confidentiality can give you the leverage to negotiate, the freedom to grow, and the power to pivot when you need to.

The Value of Silence: Why Financial Confidentiality Matters

When you're building something big, people watch. Whether it's competitors, partners, or even people close to you, everyone wants to gauge where you're at. Are you flush with cash or running lean? Are you self-funded or investor-backed? And more importantly, what do those answers mean for them? Every financial detail you let slip shifts your perceived power and vulnerability, and savvy players will use that to their advantage.

For an entrepreneur, keeping your financials close isn't just about avoiding envy or nosy questions; it's about maintaining control. When you keep quiet, you're in the driver's seat. You get to decide when to expand, who to partner with, and how to approach negotiations. It's a power move that lets you stay flexible and act on your terms. After all, if no one knows what you have, no one can manipulate what you lack.

Take the story of the co-founders of Warby Parker, a business launched with the simple premise of selling stylish, affordable eyewear directly to consumers. Warby Parker's founders were strategic in keeping their finances confidential as they bootstrapped the company and entered a competitive market dominated by big players like Luxottica. By controlling what they revealed, they kept their power close, protecting themselves from both competitors and copycats. Their discretion allowed them to grow quietly, avoid unnecessary scrutiny, and carve out a unique position in the market.

The Risk of Transparency: How Oversharing Can Undermine Your Business

In an age where transparency is often seen as a positive value, keeping quiet about finances can feel counterintuitive. We're taught to "own our successes" and "be open" about our numbers. But in the world of business, oversharing can be risky. Here's why: when your financials are out in the open, they shape perceptions, and not always in ways you can control.

For a growing company, revealing too much too soon can lead to issues like inflated expectations. Imagine sharing early success numbers only to hit a slow season or unexpected dip. Suddenly, people who supported you because they believed you were a "sure thing" might doubt your stability, even if your numbers are in line with normal growth patterns. That uncertainty can drive away investors, cause loyal customers to lose confidence, and even push talented employees to look elsewhere.

Consider Sarah Kauss, founder of S'well. She bootstrapped her business from the start, launching with a goal of reducing plastic bottle usage through sustainable, stylish water bottles. From day one, she was careful about what financial details she revealed, especially as she grew from a small startup to a globally recognized brand. By keeping her numbers tight, she kept competitors guessing and controlled her brand narrative. People didn't focus on how much capital she had; they focused on the product she was bringing to market, the story she was telling, and the impact she was aiming to make. Financial discretion let her shape public perception without the distractions of financial speculation.

Building Credibility Through Strategic Silence

Keeping financials confidential isn't just about self-protection; it's also a credibility-builder. When you aren't flaunting your finances, people don't see you as a target or a braggart. Instead, they view you as focused, professional, and secure in what you're building. Silence implies that you're in control, that you don't need external validation, and that your focus is on the work, not on showing off.

Consider Jay-Z in the early stages of his career as a businessman. He didn't start out broadcasting his net worth or flaunting every acquisition. Instead, he built quietly, with an eye on the long game, keeping his moves under the radar until they were fully realized. By the time the public caught on, his empire was too solid to be undermined. This approach isn't just about power; it's about demonstrating to stakeholders that you're here to stay, that your focus is on building something substantial.

Managing Perceptions: Silence as a Shield

There's a saying in business: "Perception is reality." And when it comes to money, people's perceptions are often skewed by what they think they know. If you're too open, you give people more room to form opinions — and those opinions can create their own challenges. Whether they think you have more than you do or assume you're struggling, managing these narratives can distract from your real work. Silence, then, becomes a tool for shaping perception. When people don't know the full picture, they can't make assumptions, and that lack of certainty works to your advantage.

For instance, in the world of startups, founders are often judged by how much capital they've raised. But founders like Mailchimp's Ben Chestnut and Dan Kurzius have shown the power of staying financially private. Mailchimp was bootstrapped, and while other startups were touting funding rounds and valuations, Mailchimp was quietly building. By not engaging in the hype, they stayed focused on creating a profitable, sustainable company that eventually grew into one of the biggest names in email marketing. Their decision to keep finances close allowed them to avoid the pressure of external expectations and stay true to their vision.

Practical Steps to Maintain Financial Confidentiality

Keeping financials confidential doesn't mean being secretive to a fault. Here are some actionable steps to help you protect your financial privacy while still engaging stakeholders effectively:

Establish Boundaries Early: Let partners, employees, and investors know what kind of financial information will be shared and what won't. Clarity up front avoids misunderstandings and sets expectations.

Control Your Narrative: When you share financial information, do so on your terms. Highlight metrics that reflect your goals (such as growth rate or customer retention) instead of focusing solely on revenue or funding levels.

Use NDAs When Necessary: For high-stakes partnerships, consider using non-disclosure agreements to protect sensitive financial details. This way, you share what's essential without risking exposure.

Share Selectively in Stages: If financial updates are necessary, provide them in stages or in ranges instead of exact figures. This keeps people informed without giving away every detail.

Develop a Strong Brand Story: A compelling brand narrative shifts the focus from your finances to your mission, your values, and the quality of your product. Let your brand do the talking so your finances don't have to.

When to Open Up — and How Much to Reveal

While keeping financials confidential is generally wise, there are times when selective transparency can work to your advantage. In certain fundraising rounds or major partnership negotiations, providing a limited glimpse into your financial health can build trust and credibility. The key is to share strategically — enough to show strength and potential, but not so much that you lose control of the narrative.

Take Apple as a prime example. Apple doesn't publicly break down every detail of its financials but shares enough to inspire confidence. By selectively disclosing product margins, revenue growth, and market expansion, they maintain investor confidence without exposing themselves to unnecessary scrutiny.

Embracing the Long Game

Confidentiality is a long game, one that pays dividends as your business grows. When you stay quiet about your finances, you're not just protecting yourself from potential challenges — you're giving yourself the space to grow without the added pressures of public opinion. And that space is invaluable.

As we move into the next chapter, we'll explore the importance of guarding your strategy. Just as with your finances, your plans and intentions don't need to be public knowledge until you're ready to move. Because in the game of business, sometimes silence speaks louder than words.

Staying Under the Radar: Growing with Discretion

Growing a business often comes with the urge to showcase every win, every milestone, and every breakthrough. It's tempting to celebrate financial successes publicly — a big funding round, impressive quarterly profits, or record-breaking sales. But the truth is, the most successful players know that discretion is essential in early stages. Broadcasting each accomplishment can invite competition, raise expectations, or even lure potential detractors who'd rather see you fail.

One example of this comes from the fashion industry with the brand Supreme. Supreme built a global reputation not just for its exclusive designs but for its exclusivity and secrecy around its business operations. Financial details weren't leaked or flaunted. By staying under the radar, Supreme maintained an image of scarcity and mystique that added to the brand's allure. Its finances weren't a matter of public discussion until it was in a strong enough position to make announcements that only added value to its image, like its major acquisition by VF Corp. This choice to keep its financials close and grow without the pressure of public opinion was a key part of Supreme's long-term brand success.

Avoiding the "Money Talks" Trap

In the startup world, there's often pressure to flaunt capital and demonstrate growth early on. In Silicon Valley and beyond, funding rounds are broadcasted as a sign of success, and many founders feel pressured to join the chorus. But the reality is that funding is just one piece of the puzzle. Successful founders know that true sustainability is measured not by the money you raise but by the stability and scalability of your model. Money can buy resources, but it can't build resilience. Founders who understand this are less likely to fall into the "money talks" trap and instead focus on building a business that's strong from the inside out.

Etsy, the e-commerce marketplace for handmade goods, is a powerful case in point. When Etsy was in its early stages, founder Rob Kalin made a deliberate choice to focus on building a sustainable business model before chasing endless funding rounds. Rather than broadcasting every financial win, Kalin and his team focused on creating a loyal community and a high-quality user experience. By staying focused on building strong operations, Etsy grew at a natural pace, attracting users who appreciated its unique, personal touch. Eventually, this focus on organic growth and self-sustaining revenue streams paid off, allowing Etsy to IPO and expand with an audience and reputation solidly in place.

The Benefits of Flying Under the Radar

Financial discretion doesn't just protect your current status; it opens doors to unexpected advantages. When your financial status isn't public knowledge, you can build relationships, explore partnerships, and take calculated risks without the pressure of public opinion. Competitors aren't sizing you up based on an arbitrary valuation, and partners aren't forming expectations based on media headlines. In business, less information often means more control, and the ability to navigate with freedom can be priceless.

For example, Spanx founder Sara Blakely famously kept her business finances private for years, even as the brand grew exponentially. By keeping Spanx's financials close, Blakely was able to reinvest profits strategically, adapt her business model as needed, and take risks without worrying about how investors or the public might perceive her choices. Her decision to fly under the radar gave her the freedom to experiment, leading Spanx to become a household name and giving Blakely full ownership and control over her company's destiny.

Confidentiality and Competitor Advantage

In a competitive landscape, disclosing financials can tip off rivals, signaling when you're flush with resources and ready to expand or when you might be vulnerable. Competitors often pounce when they sense weakness or a funding shortage. But when you keep finances private, you're less predictable, and that unpredictability can become a strategic advantage.

Apple, for instance, has historically been highly secretive about its financial details regarding specific products, keeping competitors guessing about its next moves. This confidentiality has helped Apple retain a reputation for innovation and allowed the company to pivot in unexpected directions, such as when it moved from a computer company to a smartphone and tech ecosystem powerhouse. Apple's silence around its finances and plans keeps competitors off balance, creating an air of anticipation that fuels demand.

Knowing When to Speak

While keeping financials confidential is crucial, there are moments when strategic transparency can work to your advantage. Selectively sharing key financials at the right time can build investor confidence, attract new talent, or solidify partnerships. But the key is in the timing and the level of detail. Transparency should serve a purpose, not appease curiosity.

For instance, let's consider Beyoncé's 2013 self-titled album release. She surprised the world by dropping a complete, unannounced album overnight, keeping the entire project under wraps until it was ready for the public. She didn't need to tease singles or hype the release with marketing; she let the product speak for itself. Beyoncé's silence before the album release kept expectations neutral, but when the album dropped, the demand was explosive. This approach can be applied to finances in business — reveal them strategically, at the moment when they add the most value to your position.

Balancing Confidentiality with Credibility

Sometimes, financial confidentiality can raise questions, especially when it comes to attracting investors or key partners. Knowing how to balance silence with credibility can help you navigate these situations. If you're seeking outside funding or forming strategic alliances, it's essential to present your business as transparent but focused. Instead of raw numbers, focus on growth metrics, customer satisfaction, and team strength — factors that are indicators of a healthy business without exposing every detail of your finances.

Oprah Winfrey leveraged this strategy in building her brand and business empire. She was clear about her mission and her commitment to quality, values that her audience and business partners could rely on. But Winfrey rarely shared details about her personal finances, and instead built a brand rooted in her personal values and vision. Her discretion added to her mystique, creating a brand synonymous with integrity, growth, and impact. This balance of selective transparency allowed her to protect her personal financial interests while building a business that inspired trust and loyalty.

Building Trust Through Consistency, Not Disclosure

In business, trust is everything. But trust isn't built through sharing every detail of your finances; it's built through consistent action, delivering on promises, and maintaining a high standard. When people see that you're reliable and that you stay focused on your mission, they trust you — even if they don't know every figure in your bank account. Trust grows from showing, not telling.

For example, Jeff Bezos didn't build Amazon's reputation by sharing its financials from the get-go. In fact, Amazon operated at a loss for years. But Bezos focused on reinvesting every dollar into building a superior customer experience, and his consistency paid off. Today, Amazon's reputation as a trusted service and its relentless focus on the customer is so strong that the public trusts the company's financial standing almost by default. Bezos didn't need to prove it through numbers; he did it through actions.

Protecting Your Financial Privacy in the Digital Age

In today's digital world, keeping finance confidential is even more challenging. Investors, competitors, and even customers often want insight into your revenue, growth, and financial health. But digital presence doesn't have to mean full disclosure. Tools like selective online reporting, strategic public relations, and targeted investor communications can help you control the narrative and share only what's necessary.

Online platforms can provide opportunities to showcase your growth without exposing your financials. For example, metrics like customer engagement rates, product adoption, and market share growth are powerful indicators that tell a story of success without disclosing every dollar. This method allows you to stay transparent without giving up your edge, keeping your business agile and secure.

A Commandment for Longevity

Ultimately, financial confidentiality is about playing the long game. It's about understanding that business is a marathon, not a sprint, and that every move you make adds to your reputation and legacy. When you keep your financials close, you're investing in the freedom to grow, to learn, and to pivot as you see fit. It's about staying agile in a world that's quick to judge and quicker to compete.

The first commandment teaches us the value of controlling what others see. It's a lesson in holding back, staying sharp, and setting boundaries around what's yours. It's about making moves with purpose, unbothered by outside expectations. Financial discretion is power — a power that lets you focus on the hustle without the noise.

As we move into the next chapter, we'll look at the second commandment: Guard Your Strategy. Just as with your finances, your plans and moves don't need to be known until they're ready to drop. In the game of business, a quiet strategy is sometimes the loudest statement you can make. Turn the page, and let's break down what it means to keep your next move under wraps.

Chapter 2: Guard Your Strategy

"Never let 'em know your next move." — Notorious B.I.G.

If there's one thing a hustler knows, it's that plans work best when kept close. Biggie's second commandment is a reminder that letting people know your next move takes away your advantage. In business, the power of your strategy often lies in its mystery. Just like in the streets, when everyone knows what you're about to do, they can anticipate, copy, or even sabotage your efforts. Keeping your strategy under wraps gives you control over when and how you reveal it, positioning you to act on your terms.

This chapter is about understanding the value of a quiet, calculated approach to your business moves. We'll explore why guarding your strategy is essential, how it can shape perceptions, and the ways it sets you apart from competitors who might be too quick to show their hand. Through real-life examples, we'll see how leaders have thrived by holding their cards close, only making their plans public when it was time to execute. Whether you're building a new product, entering a new market, or forming strategic partnerships, your advantage is in your silence.

Playing the Long Game: Why Strategy Should Be Private

In business, the long game is about building success that's sustainable, impactful, and resilient. But this approach requires patience and, often, secrecy. By holding back on revealing every move, you give yourself room to pivot, adapt, and refine. When your strategy isn't on public display, you're free to adjust without external pressure or judgment.

People only see the finished result — the moment you're ready for the reveal.

Consider the story of Netflix. In its early days, Netflix was a DVD rental company, competing with the likes of Blockbuster. But while Blockbuster was busy flexing its dominance in brick-and-mortar stores, Netflix was planning its pivot to streaming, a move that would change the entertainment industry forever. They didn't announce their streaming plans years in advance. They quietly invested in the technology, refined the service, and then, when the time was right, they launched. Netflix's strategy didn't just surprise competitors — it shifted the entire industry. By guarding their next move, Netflix was able to lead with impact, positioning itself as the future of media.

This approach is especially powerful when entering a crowded market. If you're stepping into an industry where others already dominate, silence can protect you as you build, letting you perfect your offer and refine your approach before making a splash. When you're ready to reveal, you come out strong, confident, and with a unique position that no one anticipated. Keeping quiet on your strategy while you're still developing gives you a head start, making your reveal all the more impactful when it's time to launch.

Why Oversharing Your Plans Can Backfire

In today's world of social media and constant connectivity, there's a temptation to share every step of your journey. People want to announce new ventures, talk about what's next, and generate buzz. But that buzz can come with a price. When you overshare your plans, you expose yourself to critiques, distractions, and expectations that can hinder your ability to focus and execute. You've let the world in, and now everyone feels entitled to an opinion.

Tesla CEO Elon Musk is an example of how oversharing can sometimes backfire. Musk is known for his ambitious plans, and he often announces them through social media, from launching new Tesla models to plans for colonizing Mars. While Musk's transparency is part of his brand, it has sometimes worked against him. There have been instances where his public announcements have led to shareholder doubt, regulatory scrutiny, and unrealistic public expectations. Sharing the vision is one thing; sharing the play-by-play can sometimes add unnecessary pressure to deliver on every word.

Think of it this way: when you publicly commit to a move before you're fully prepared to back it up, you're not just exposing yourself to judgment — you're risking your credibility. Everyone loves a big announcement, but without the ability to back it up in real time, an announcement can easily turn into disappointment. When you talk less and deliver more, you build a reputation based on action, not hype. The most successful leaders know how to keep excitement in check until the moment their moves are ready to be seen.

The Art of Silence in Business

Silence in business isn't about withholding information to be mysterious; it's about controlling the flow of information. When you speak only, when necessary, people learn to listen. Your moves hold weight because you're not constantly telegraphing your intentions. You choose when and how to share, making each announcement count. This kind of controlled silence creates curiosity and respect, giving your strategy an edge.

Apple, for instance, is famous for its tight-lipped approach to product releases and strategic decisions. Known for holding back details until launch day, Apple has built an aura of anticipation and exclusivity around its brand. People don't just want to buy Apple products; they want to experience the unveiling of those products. Apple's strategic silence keeps competitors guessing and leaves consumers eager to see what's next, making each announcement an event. By guarding its strategy and making each release count, Apple doesn't just sell products — it sells experiences.

In your own business, silence can be just as powerful. Holding back on sharing every detail creates intrigue, and that intrigue builds authority. Your audience begins to expect results from you, not just announcements. And in a marketplace where every business is competing for attention, the ability to control your story and reveal only what matters is a strategic advantage.

Using Strategy as a Shield

When competitors don't know your next move, you have the power of unpredictability on your side. In a market where imitation is common, staying quiet about your plans can prevent copycats from hijacking your ideas. The less they know, the harder it is for them to react. In competitive industries, silence is a shield that protects your innovation.

Think of Coca-Cola. For decades, Coca-Cola has kept its formula a tightly guarded secret, known by only a handful of people. While competitors have tried to replicate its taste, the mystique around its "secret recipe" has added to Coca-Cola's brand value, making the product as much about exclusivity as it is about taste. This decision not to reveal everything not only prevents imitation but builds loyalty — people buy into the legacy and mystery as much as the drink itself.

Your business strategy may not be as iconic as Coca-Cola's formula, but the principle holds true: when you keep competitors out of your plans, they're left to guess. And that guessing game keeps them on the defensive, giving you the freedom to focus on growth without looking over your shoulder. The less predictable you are, the harder it is for anyone to stay ahead of you.

The Power of the Surprise Move

Holding back on your strategy doesn't just protect you; it allows you to create powerful moments of surprise. When you make an unexpected move, you control the narrative and force others to react on your terms. Surprising your audience can create momentum and increase impact, establishing your brand as innovative and forward-thinking.

Consider Beyoncé's self-titled album drop in 2013. She released it with zero promotion, no marketing campaign, and no hint of what was coming. The move shocked the music industry and delighted fans, creating an explosive response that traditional album releases rarely achieve. Beyoncé's surprise strategy wasn't just about generating buzz; it showed her control over her craft and redefined how artists could connect with their audiences. In business, the element of surprise can be just as powerful, allowing you to make a statement that echoes long after the initial move.

The element of surprise isn't limited to big releases; it's a powerful strategy you can weave into every stage of your growth. For example, if you're rolling out a new product line, consider the impact of a sudden reveal. Let your loyal customers be the first to know, then let the market catch up. The effect of surprising people with fully realized work, ready to be bought, tried, or experienced, solidifies your reputation for quality and foresight. You're no longer just a brand; you're a brand with a plan — a brand with control.

Building Your Strategy Fortress: Practical Tips

Guarding your strategy isn't just a mindset; it's a skill you can develop. Here are some actionable steps to help you build a "strategy fortress," protecting your plans until they're ready for the world:

Limit Your Inner Circle: Share your strategic plans only with essential team members. The fewer people who know the details, the fewer chances there are for leaks. Build trust within this circle and ensure they understand the importance of confidentiality.

Time Your Announcements Carefully: Timing is everything. Announce plans only when you're ready to act on them. Early announcements can invite feedback and pressure that may distract from your actual execution.

Emphasize Execution Over Talk: Let your actions speak louder than your words. If you're focused on strategy, your time is better spent executing than explaining. When people see results, your work speaks for itself.

Control the Narrative: When you do announce, be in control of the narrative. Decide what details you'll share and how you'll frame your message. This allows you to guide the story, protecting the parts of your strategy that still need time to develop.

Create Decoy Moves: Sometimes, a little misdirection can keep competitors off your trail. By focusing attention on one aspect of your business, you can keep your real plans hidden until they're ready for prime time.

Silence as a Culture

Incorporating silence into your business strategy goes beyond individual moves; it becomes part of your company's culture. When your team understands that strategy isn't for public consumption, they align with the same sense of discretion and protectiveness over your brand's moves. This culture of quiet focus can keep your team grounded, even when the industry around you is noisy.

Amazon's Jeff Bezos instilled this culture at his company, keeping the focus on customer experience rather than public strategy discussions. Amazon rarely reveals its next big project, preferring to focus on execution. This culture of "customer obsession" allows Amazon to continuously innovate without the distraction of public opinion on every move. By keeping strategy internal, Amazon stays agile and competitive, avoiding the pitfalls of overexposure.

Choosing When to Reveal

There will come a time when sharing your strategy is the right move. Whether it's a product launch, an expansion announcement, or a major partnership, a well-timed reveal can amplify your impact. The key is to choose moments where sharing serves a purpose beyond publicity — when it strengthens relationships, drives customer interest, or solidifies your brand's credibility.

Take the example of Nike. When they launched their "Just Do It" campaign, they didn't announce a shift in strategy; they simply released a bold, impactful message that aligned with the company's values. The campaign wasn't just marketing; it was a strategic move that spoke directly to their audience, unifying the brand's voice and vision. Nike's calculated reveal wasn't about showing off; it was about creating a moment that reinforced their brand's strength.

Protecting the Blueprint for Long-Term Success

In the end, guarding your strategy is about laying a foundation for sustainable success. When you control the flow of information, you protect your focus, shield your innovation, and build a brand that people respect. The game of business is unpredictable, and keeping your moves close lets you stay one step ahead, adapting as the landscape changes without the added pressure of public scrutiny.

This second commandment isn't just a rule; it's a discipline. It's about recognizing the power of silence and using it as a tool to build something bigger than buzz. By guarding your strategy, you're preparing to win, setting yourself up for moves that make a real impact when they land. Silence, in this sense, becomes a weapon — one that keeps you sharp, steady, and always ready to move.

As we move forward, we'll dive into the next commandment: Trust but Verify. Because while your silence is a strength, the people you choose to work with can make or break the strategy you guard. It's about understanding who's in your circle, and who truly has your back. Turn the page, and let's explore the art of building trust without giving it blindly.

Chapter 3: Trust but Verify

"Never trust nobody." — *Notorious B.I.G.*

Trust is a powerful thing. In business, like in life, people often say that relationships are everything. The partnerships you form, the team you build, and the mentors you choose can make or break your journey. But trust, as Biggie warned, can't be given freely. In a world where everyone is playing their own game, trust needs to be earned — and verified. Whether you're forging alliances, hiring employees, or signing deals, having a solid framework for evaluating trust is a skill every entrepreneur needs.

This chapter is about striking the balance between connection and caution, about being open to collaboration but staying grounded in due diligence. We'll explore why skepticism is as valuable as openness, how to verify trust without losing authenticity, and how building relationships strategically can add resilience to your business. Real-life stories will show us that trusting carefully doesn't mean missing out on valuable partnerships; it means safeguarding what you've worked hard to build.

Why Trust Is a Risk

In a fast-moving business landscape, trust isn't something to take lightly. While building a strong network is essential, every person you bring into your inner circle impacts your business. And every time you enter a new partnership, you're putting your name, your brand, and your credibility on the line. Trusting the wrong person can lead to financial losses, reputational damage, and even legal battles.

Look at the story of Theranos, once a promising startup in the biotech world led by Elizabeth Holmes. Investors, employees, and clients trusted Holmes's vision and promises without verifying the company's actual capabilities. The result was a massive scandal that led to millions lost, careers damaged, and public trust in the industry shaken. Theranos's story serves as a cautionary tale about blind trust, a reminder that no matter how charismatic or convincing someone may be, trust must be balanced with verification.

In business, it's essential to evaluate the motives, intentions, and track records of everyone you work with. That doesn't mean assuming the worst in people, but it does mean staying alert and doing your homework. Building relationships based on true understanding and verified alignment makes for a more resilient, reliable network.

The Importance of "Due Diligence"

In the business world, the term due diligence refers to the process of thoroughly investigating a person, company, or deal before making a commitment. It's a structured approach to confirming that someone is what they claim to be and that they bring value, not risk. Due diligence helps you cut through the surface and see the details that truly matter. For instance, a new vendor might have an impressive portfolio, but a quick investigation could reveal a history of missed deadlines or quality issues.

Take the example of Nike and its strategic partnerships. Before Nike collaborates with a new athlete, influencer, or brand, it conducts rigorous due diligence, checking everything from reputational history to future goals. Nike's careful approach to partnerships is why they've avoided the high-profile controversies that have tripped up other brands. They don't just trust an individual or company based on a good pitch; they verify alignment with their own values and standards.

When you're bringing someone into your circle, whether it's a business partner or an investor, performing due diligence is an act of protection. It shields your brand, your vision, and your assets from unnecessary risk. It's not about skepticism; it's about security.

Building Trust Step-by-Step

Trust can't be rushed. When you're developing a business relationship, approaching trust as a gradual process can save you from costly mistakes. Here's a practical breakdown of how you can build trust thoughtfully without rushing into commitments.

Start Small: Don't jump into high-stakes collaborations with new connections. Begin with small projects, limited partnerships, or short-term contracts. This allows both parties to demonstrate reliability and understand each other's work style before committing to larger initiatives.

Set Clear Expectations: Transparency in expectations is key. Lay out deliverables, deadlines, and goals clearly so that both sides know what's required. Ambiguity breeds misunderstanding and mistrust, while clarity builds a foundation for collaboration.

Check References and Past Work: Whenever possible, take time to verify the past work of those you're considering for collaboration. Speak with past clients or colleagues, review their portfolio, and get a sense of their reputation in the industry.

Evaluate Motives: Understand why the other party wants to collaborate. Are they genuinely interested in a mutually beneficial partnership, or are they looking to benefit from your brand without contributing in return?

Be Open but Guarded: Building trust doesn't mean being closed off. You can be open in communication and generous with support while still being cautious about giving away sensitive information or control.

By taking a gradual approach to trust, you protect your business from potentially harmful alliances while building relationships that are solid and sustainable.

Recognizing Red Flags

Even when someone seems like a great fit, there may be red flags that suggest otherwise. Recognizing these signs early can prevent you from entering a partnership that could drain resources, time, and morale. Here are some common red flags to watch for:

Inconsistent Communication: If a potential partner is slow to respond, doesn't answer questions directly, or frequently changes their story, these are indicators of unreliability.

Unclear Financials: If they hesitate to provide information about their finances or past projects, it could mean they're hiding something. In business, transparency is a two-way street.

Over-Promising: If someone promises outcomes that seem too good to be true, they probably are. High achievers set realistic expectations and back them up with evidence, not hype.

Shifting Blame: Be wary of people who constantly blame others for past failures. A trustworthy partner takes accountability and learns from mistakes.

Red flags don't necessarily mean someone is deceitful, but they should be a signal to proceed with caution. Sometimes, it's best to take a step back and reassess before moving forward.

Case Study: Google and Android

One example of a partnership based on trust, caution, and careful verification is Google's acquisition of Android. When Google first considered acquiring the Android team, it wasn't widely known, and the technology itself was still in development. Rather than rushing into a partnership, Google spent time evaluating Android's long-term potential, vision, and compatibility with its own plans for mobile.

Google's strategic patience paid off. They saw value in Android's potential and decided to bring the team onboard, ultimately leading to the launch of the Android operating system, now the most widely used mobile OS in the world. By moving slowly, building trust step-by-step, and verifying Android's capabilities, Google established a partnership that became a cornerstone of its mobile success. This approach shows that trust, when combined with careful vetting, can yield powerful, long-lasting results.

The Value of Boundaries

Building trust doesn't mean giving people access to every aspect of your business. Establishing boundaries, both personal and professional, is key to maintaining control over your work and protecting your interests. When people know where the lines are, they're less likely to overstep, and you're less likely to feel exposed.

For example, if you're bringing on a new partner, setting boundaries around decision-making can prevent future conflicts. Determine who has final say on specific issues, agree on financial limits, and define areas where each partner has autonomy. These boundaries don't limit trust; they create a framework within which trust can grow without compromising the business.

Building a Trustworthy Network

Trust is a two-way street. While it's important to verify the intentions of others, building your own reputation as someone who can be trusted is equally valuable. When you're seen as reliable, consistent, and fair, people are more likely to bring opportunities, refer clients, and recommend you to others in their network. A reputation for integrity attracts the right people and naturally filters out those with less honest intentions.

One way to build this reputation is by creating a "trustworthy network" — a circle of collaborators, advisors, and mentors who know your values, respect your vision, and are committed to mutual growth. Building a network like this requires intention; it means choosing people who align with your goals and who bring value, insights, and a willingness to grow together.

When Oprah Winfrey first started the OWN network, she knew the importance of surrounding herself with people she could rely on. Winfrey built a trusted network of advisors and content creators who understood her vision and respected her leadership style. By carefully choosing her circle, she created a supportive network that helped her bring her vision to life, a testament to how trustworthiness on both sides can propel a venture forward.

Practical Tips for Trust-Building in Business

Building trust carefully and strategically isn't complicated, but it does require discipline. Here are some actionable tips to build a strong foundation of trust with those you work with:

Keep Your Word: This may sound simple, but consistency is the best way to build trust. Follow through on commitments, meet deadlines, and deliver what you promise. Reliability forms the backbone of trust.

Communicate Transparently: Open communication builds confidence. If you encounter challenges or delays, let people know early. Being upfront about setbacks shows integrity and reassures others that you respect their time.

Respect Confidentiality: Show that you can be trusted with sensitive information. When someone shares private details, keep them confidential. This sets a standard of trust and reciprocation.

Be Open to Feedback: Show others that you're willing to improve. Accept constructive criticism and demonstrate that you're open to making adjustments when needed. A collaborative approach to feedback fosters mutual trust.

Document Agreements: Put agreements in writing, whether they're formal contracts or simple email confirmations. This not only provides clarity but demonstrates professionalism and foresight.

Knowing When to Walk Away

Sometimes, trust doesn't develop the way you hope. When the red flags pile up, or when someone isn't meeting the standards of reliability, it's essential to know when to walk away. Ending a business relationship can be challenging, but sticking with someone who isn't trustworthy is often more damaging in the long run.

The WeWork saga is a case in point. Investors initially trusted WeWork's founder, Adam Neumann, but as red flags emerged — from reckless spending to questionable leadership practices — they realized the partnership was too risky. Eventually, major investors pulled out, leading to Neumann's ouster, and restructuring of the company. This decision to walk away, though difficult, allowed WeWork to stabilize and salvage its brand.

Walking away doesn't mean failure; it means protecting your business from people or situations that don't align with your values or vision. Sometimes, maintaining trust in yourself and your goals means letting go of those who can't meet the standard.

The Strength of Verified Trust

In the end, trusting wisely is about striking a balance between openness and protection. Relationships can propel your business forward, but only when they're based on genuine understanding, mutual respect, and verified intentions. Trusting others is valuable, but trusting the process of verification is what keeps your business steady, even when challenges arise.

As we move to the next chapter, remember that building trust isn't about limiting opportunities; it's about securing them. In Chapter 4, we'll look at the importance of keeping personal and professional boundaries. While trust is a necessary ingredient in business, boundaries allow you to navigate challenges without losing yourself or compromising your vision. Turn the page, and let's explore how setting boundaries empowers your growth.

Chapter 4: Separate Personal from Professional

"Never get high on your own supply." — *Notorious B.I.G.*

When Biggie laid down this commandment, he wasn't just talking about products; he was making a point about self-discipline. In the hustle, getting too deep in what you're selling can lead to a loss of control, blurring the line between work and personal life. This same rule applies to business: keep a clear line between the personal and the professional. Mixing the two can lead to burnout, financial trouble, and lost credibility.

In this chapter, we dive into the art of boundaries, examining why separating your personal life from your business life can be a game-changer. Building a business is a grind, often requiring all of you. But when you lose sight of the boundary between personal and professional, you risk losing yourself in the work, making decisions that aren't strategic, and even jeopardizing the legacy you're building. Here, we'll explore how maintaining that boundary keeps your mind clear, your finances healthy, and your relationships steady.

The Power of Boundaries

Boundaries are often misunderstood. People see them as walls, restrictions on how they can operate. But in reality, boundaries are freedom. They give you the structure to perform at your best without sacrificing your health, relationships, or well-being. In business, boundaries aren't just helpful; they're essential. They protect your time, your focus, and your resources.

Take Elon Musk, known for his relentless work ethic but also criticized for blurring the lines between his personal and professional lives. By taking on intense workloads and bringing personal struggles into the business arena, he's faced challenges that have affected his public image, relationships, and even shareholder confidence. Musk's example serves as a reminder that ambition, when unchecked, can turn into a double-edged sword. A lack of boundaries might lead to success, but at what cost?

Boundaries keep you centered. They remind you that your business is something you're building, not something that owns you. When you create a healthy distance, you give yourself the freedom to make objective decisions and maintain a balanced perspective. Your business benefits from this balance, as do you.

Protecting Your Personal Finances

One of the biggest challenges for entrepreneurs is separating personal finances from business finances. The temptation to dip into business accounts to cover personal expenses, or vice versa, is real — especially in the early stages when cash flow is unpredictable. But mixing personal and business finances can be a slippery slope that leads to financial chaos.

Consider the example of entrepreneurs who invest their life savings into their startup without separating their personal assets. While the initial commitment might seem like a necessary risk, it can backfire if the business encounters financial difficulties. Without a clear boundary between personal and business finances, you risk losing personal assets, like savings or even property, if the business goes through a rough patch.

Setting up separate bank accounts and using dedicated credit cards for business expenses are practical steps that reinforce this boundary. Having clear distinctions in your financial life helps you manage cash flow effectively, monitor business expenses accurately, and keep personal finances safe from the ups and downs of entrepreneurship. Think of it as a protective measure, not a restriction.

Managing Emotional Investment

Building a business is an emotional journey. You pour time, passion, and energy into making your vision a reality, and it's natural to feel personally connected to its success or failure. But when you get too emotionally invested, you can lose objectivity, making decisions based on feelings rather than facts.

Jeff Bezos, founder of Amazon, is an example of someone who mastered this balance. Despite Amazon's explosive growth, Bezos consistently approached business decisions with a rational, data-driven mindset. While he was undoubtedly invested in Amazon's success, he maintained enough distance to make clear-headed choices, even when they were difficult. Bezos's decision to sell his first company, a successful but limited startup, was driven by logic, not attachment. His ability to separate his emotions from his business laid the foundation for Amazon's future growth.

Maintaining an emotional boundary helps you stay resilient in the face of setbacks. Instead of taking every challenge or failure personally, you learn to view them as part of the process. This balance keeps you flexible and focused on growth, allowing you to make the best decisions for your business without letting emotions cloud your judgment.

Balancing Personal Relationships

Entrepreneurs often struggle with balancing their business commitments and personal relationships. When you're deeply invested in your work, it's easy to let relationships slide, rationalizing it as "necessary sacrifice." But business success isn't just about profit; it's about building a life that's rich in experience and connection. Neglecting relationships in the name of business often leads to regrets down the line.

Richard Branson, founder of the Virgin Group, is a prime example of someone who has prioritized balance. Despite his ambitious pursuits, Branson has consistently made family and personal relationships a priority. He credits his family support as crucial to his success, and his ability to step back from business when needed has helped him maintain a healthy personal life. For Branson, family time isn't a luxury; it's a necessity that keeps him grounded and fuels his creativity.

Your personal relationships are assets, not distractions. Strong relationships support you, remind you of who you are outside of your business, and help you recharge. By setting boundaries around work hours, unplugging from devices, and dedicating time to family and friends, you maintain these relationships while pursuing your professional goals. It's not about choosing one over the other; it's about creating a lifestyle that honors both.

Avoiding Burnout

Burnout is real, and it often hits hardest when the boundary between personal and professional is blurred. When you're constantly "on" for your business, it's easy to fall into a cycle of overwork, where you're unable to truly relax. Burnout doesn't just affect your productivity; it impacts your mental health, creativity, and overall quality of life.

Arianna Huffington, founder of The Huffington Post, experienced severe burnout that led her to re-evaluate her relationship with work. After collapsing from exhaustion, she became an advocate for work-life balance and launched Thrive Global, a platform dedicated to helping people prevent burnout. Huffington's wake-up call shifted her perspective, teaching her the importance of rest, boundaries, and creating space for personal well-being.

Setting boundaries around work hours, taking time off, and prioritizing sleep and relaxation can prevent burnout. When you recognize the warning signs and respect your limits, you're able to bring your best self to your business and avoid the pitfalls of overextending.

Creating a Workspace Boundary

Working from home has become common, but it can blur the line between personal and professional life. Without a clear separation between work and home, it's easy to feel like you're always on the clock. Creating a designated workspace, even if it's just a corner in a small apartment, helps you mentally switch between work mode and personal time.

Tech entrepreneur Jack Dorsey, co-founder of Twitter and Square, maintains a strict routine to separate his work and personal life. Dorsey's structured schedule includes regular breaks, designated work hours, and even "theme days" to focus on specific aspects of his businesses. This approach not only enhances productivity but also prevents work from encroaching on his personal life.

By setting up a designated workspace and establishing rituals that mark the beginning and end of the workday, you create a mental boundary that helps you transition in and out of work mode. This structure enables you to fully engage in your work when you're "at the office" and enjoy personal time when the workday is done.

Learning to Say No

For entrepreneurs, saying "no" can feel counterintuitive. When you're building something, every opportunity seems valuable, every connection important. But saying "yes" to everything can lead to a cluttered calendar and stretched resources. Setting boundaries often means learning to say "no" to projects, clients, or tasks that don't align with your priorities.

Oprah Winfrey famously struggled with this early in her career. She wanted to help everyone, to be everything to everyone. But over time, she realized that saying "yes" to everything was costing her peace of mind and focus. Oprah learned the power of a well-placed "no," using it to protect her energy, her schedule, and her vision.

Saying no doesn't mean closing yourself off to growth; it means valuing your time and energy enough to reserve them for what truly matters. When you set boundaries around what you'll take on, you ensure that every commitment is purposeful, leaving room for what aligns with your goals and values.

Practical Tips for Keeping Personal and Professional Separate

Keeping personal and professional boundaries strong isn't always easy, especially in the fast-paced world of business. Here are practical ways to maintain these boundaries effectively:

Create Separate Bank Accounts: Use different accounts for personal and business finances. This makes it easier to track expenses, simplifies taxes, and keeps your personal funds safe from business fluctuations.

Set a Schedule: Designate work hours and commit to unplugging after a certain time. This helps you maintain a sense of routine and ensures you have dedicated personal time.

Limit Device Access: Use different devices for work and personal tasks if possible, or at least separate your work-related apps and personal apps. This physical boundary helps you disengage from work.

Schedule Personal Time: Put family events, hobbies, and self-care on your calendar just like business meetings. Making time for yourself and your loved ones is as important as any business task.

Document Policies: Write down your boundaries in a document, like a personal manifesto. Include rules like "no business talk after 8 PM" or "Saturdays are family-only." This serves as a reminder to honor your commitments to yourself.

Knowing When It's Time to Recalibrate

As your business grows, your boundaries may need adjustment. What worked in the early days may need to shift as your responsibilities change. Take time regularly to evaluate if your boundaries are working for you or if they're slipping. When you notice signs of stress, burnout, or conflict, take it as a cue to recalibrate.

Singer and entrepreneur Rihanna, known for her Fenty Beauty line, initially worked non-stop to establish her brand. But as Fenty's success grew, she began to scale back her involvement, bringing in trusted leaders to take on some responsibilities. By adjusting her role, Rihanna maintained her creative influence without sacrificing her personal time and mental health. This flexibility has allowed her to continue growing her brand while maintaining her personal life.

Adapting your boundaries as your life and business evolve is a mark of maturity. It shows that you respect both your work and your well-being enough to create a balance that works for you in the present.

Building Success Without Sacrificing Yourself

At the end of the day, building a business is about creating something meaningful — not just for others, but for yourself. By maintaining a clear line between personal and professional, you protect your peace, your purpose, and your energy. Business is a marathon, not a sprint, and longevity requires a foundation that respects all aspects of who you are.

Biggie's words remind us that even in the hustle, moderation and discipline are everything. When you honor the boundary between work and life, you set yourself up to succeed in both. In Chapter 5, we'll dig into the next commandment: Keep Home and Work Separate. Because while building a business from your passion is powerful, letting it take over your life is a risk every entrepreneur needs to guard against. Turn the page, and let's talk about how to protect what matters most.

Chapter 5: Keep Home and Work Separate

"Never sell no crack where you rest at." — Notorious B.I.G.

Biggie's fifth commandment is all about protecting your sanctuary. In his world, it meant not mixing the hustle with where you find peace and safety. In the world of business, this rule translates to keeping home and work separate — creating a boundary between where you grind and where you rest. When you blur the lines, you risk losing both your focus in business and your peace at home.

In this chapter, we'll dive into why a clear boundary between your work life and your home life is critical for long-term success. We'll explore the importance of a dedicated workspace, strategies for mentally separating work from personal life, and tips on cultivating routines that help you recharge. From the benefits of "unplugging" to the pitfalls of always working from home, we'll look at how these boundaries protect not just your productivity but your overall well-being. Let's get into it — here's how separating home and work can empower your journey.

The Cost of Mixing Work and Home

When work and home start to overlap, it doesn't just create physical chaos; it can impact your relationships, mental health, and sense of control. For entrepreneurs and business leaders, the temptation to work from anywhere is real, especially with the rise of remote work. But when your home becomes your office, there's often no end to the workday, and that constant accessibility can make it difficult to turn off.

Take the example of Marissa Mayer, former CEO of Yahoo. Known for her intense work ethic, Mayer often blurred the line between home and work, famously installing a nursery next to her office so she could work long hours. While this approach may have boosted productivity temporarily, the toll on her personal life and well-being was significant. The lack of separation between work and home led to burnout, affecting her focus and, ultimately, her career.

The truth is, when work takes over your home, it becomes nearly impossible to recharge fully. You're left in a cycle where rest is shallow, stress builds up, and productivity eventually drops. By respecting the boundary between home and work, you give yourself permission to truly rest, making you sharper and more effective when it's time to clock in.

Creating a Dedicated Workspace

One of the most practical steps you can take to separate work from home is to create a designated workspace. Even if you're working from a small apartment or a shared space, having a specific area dedicated to work can make all the difference. This physical boundary tells your brain, "This is where work happens," helping you mentally switch between productivity and relaxation.

Consider the setup of tech mogul Jack Dorsey, co-founder of Twitter and Square. Dorsey is known for his disciplined approach to work-life balance, setting up his workspace to foster focus and productivity while maintaining boundaries. By creating a structured work environment, he avoids the temptation to work from bed or lounge areas, keeping his workspace and relaxation spaces distinct. His approach shows that even in high-pressure roles, a separation between work and personal space can enhance mental clarity and efficiency.

For many, creating a dedicated workspace can be as simple as setting up a desk in the corner of a room or designating a specific chair for work tasks. When you physically leave that area, you're signaling to your mind that work is over for the day. This ritual not only increases productivity but also ensures that the rest of your home remains a place of comfort and relaxation.

Establishing Work Hours — and Sticking to Them

When you're running a business or managing a team, it's easy to feel that every hour is a potential work hour. But establishing clear work hours and respecting them is essential for maintaining a healthy boundary. Setting a start and end time for your workday creates a routine that protects your personal time and prevents work from creeping into every corner of your life.

Oprah Winfrey, an entrepreneur known for her disciplined approach to work, schedules her day with clear boundaries. Despite her success and numerous commitments, she doesn't let work interfere with her personal rituals or rest. By scheduling her day intentionally, she's able to give her full attention to each part of her life, whether she's leading a meeting or spending time in self-care.

Your hours don't have to follow a 9-to-5 schedule, but they do need to be consistent. Establish your work hours, and let your team and clients know when you're available. Once those hours are over, unplug. Turn off email notifications, log out of work apps, and allow yourself to be fully present in your personal life. This structure not only improves work-life balance but also makes your working hours more productive.

The Art of Unplugging

The digital world makes it incredibly easy to be "always on." With emails, social media notifications, and project management tools at your fingertips, it can feel impossible to fully disconnect. But unplugging is essential for maintaining boundaries, especially when work and home are in the same space.

Arianna Huffington, founder of The Huffington Post, is a champion for unplugging, especially after her own experience with burnout. She promotes a "digital detox" and encourages her team to disconnect outside of work hours to improve focus and mental health. Huffington's approach emphasizes that unplugging isn't just a luxury; it's a necessity for sustainable success.

Unplugging can be as simple as setting an "away" message on email after hours, turning off notifications on your phone, or using apps that limit screen time. By stepping away from your devices, you give your mind a chance to relax, to refocus on what truly matters, and to come back to work refreshed. Make unplugging a ritual, a commitment to yourself and your well-being.

Creating Rituals to Mark the Transition

Switching from work to personal time isn't always easy, especially when your workspace is only steps away from where you relax. Creating end-of-day rituals can help you mentally transition from work mode to personal time, giving you a sense of closure and allowing you to leave the stresses of the day behind.

Some people find that something as simple as closing a laptop, tidying up their desk, or changing into more casual clothes can signal the end of the workday. Others might take a short walk, do a quick workout, or spend a few minutes journaling about the day's successes and challenges. These rituals help create a boundary between the workday and the evening, reminding you that it's time to shift your focus.

For example, Bill Gates is known for his nightly reading ritual. Regardless of his responsibilities, Gates spends an hour each evening reading books across a range of topics, from science to history. This ritual not only helps him wind down but also stimulates his creativity, making him sharper when he returns to work. Your ritual can be as simple or elaborate as you like, as long as it helps you make a clear distinction between work and personal time.

Balancing Family Life

If you live with family or a partner, keeping work out of your home life becomes even more important. When you bring work stress or unfinished tasks into family time, it disrupts the dynamic, causing friction and resentment. Balancing family life requires clear boundaries that allow you to be fully present with loved ones.

Michelle Obama, during her time as First Lady, was intentional about protecting family time despite a demanding schedule. She made it a priority to be present with her daughters, Sasha and Malia, scheduling family dinners and quality time. Even with the weight of the White House on her shoulders, Obama showed that boundaries are essential for keeping family connections strong.

Being fully present at home starts with creating boundaries that signal to loved ones that they're a priority. This means setting a limit on work talk, respecting family routines, and ensuring that your personal life isn't overshadowed by professional demands. When your family knows that they have your undivided attention, relationships deepen, and you'll find a renewed energy that benefits both home and work.

Avoiding "Work Creep" on Weekends

For many entrepreneurs, the weekend isn't sacred — it's just another opportunity to get things done. But letting work creep into weekends can prevent you from recharging fully. Taking regular, intentional breaks is crucial for maintaining the energy and creativity needed to lead effectively. Weekends are a chance to step back, assess the bigger picture, and come back to work with a fresh perspective.

Jeff Weiner, former CEO of LinkedIn, schedules time for reflection and rest. His weekends aren't filled with work tasks but with activities that help him recharge, such as exercise, family time, and personal reflection. This balance enables him to bring his best self to work each Monday, proving that boundaries are not only beneficial but necessary for sustained leadership.

Practical Tips for Separating Home and Work

Maintaining a boundary between home and work requires commitment and practical steps. Here are some ways to create and protect that separation:

Designate a Work Zone: Set up a specific area for work, even if it's small. Avoid using personal spaces, like the bed or couch, for work tasks.

Create a Morning and Evening Routine: Structure your start and end of the day with rituals, such as a morning coffee routine or an evening walk, to signal the beginning and end of work.

Set Expectations with Family: Let family members know your work hours, and respect shared routines and activities.

Use Technology to Help You Unplug: Turn off notifications on your phone, set app usage limits, or use "Do Not Disturb" mode during non-working hours.

Plan Time Off Regularly: Make time for weekends, vacations, or even a short break during the day to recharge. Use this time to focus on non-work-related activities.

Knowing When to Reassess Your Boundaries

Over time, your business needs and personal life may shift, requiring adjustments to your boundaries. Reassessing boundaries regularly can help you stay aligned with your values and maintain balance. If you notice stress creeping back into your life or family relationships becoming strained, it might be time to adjust your boundaries.

Sheryl Sandberg, COO of Facebook, is known for her commitment to balance. When she became a mother, she shifted her boundaries, leaving the office at a specific time each day to be with her children. As her career and personal life evolved, so did her boundaries. Sandberg's approach shows that boundaries aren't rigid; they can adapt to support you in different seasons of life.

Building a Business Without Losing Your Peace

At its core, separating work from home is about preserving your peace. It's about creating a business that supports your life, not consumes it. By protecting your personal space, you gain clarity, energy, and resilience that empower you to keep building without burning out.

Biggie's words remind us to value our sanctuaries, our personal spaces, and our peace. When you honor this boundary, you set yourself up for a sustainable career and a life that's rich in meaning. In Chapter 6, we'll explore the importance of financial boundaries. Because keeping your business money separate from your personal life isn't just good practice — it's a commandment. Turn the page, and let's dive into why financial boundaries matter.

Chapter 6: Limit Reliance on Credit

"That credit? Forget it!" — *Notorious B.I.G.*

Biggie's sixth commandment is all about understanding the dangers of credit. In the world of hustling, owing people makes you vulnerable — someone else has a piece of you, a claim on your future. In business, the same principle applies. Credit can seem like a lifeline, a way to get started or expand quickly, but over-reliance on it can backfire. Debt can become a trap, eating into your cash flow, pulling your focus away from growth, and limiting your freedom to maneuver when you need it most.

This chapter will explore the role of credit in business, when it's helpful, and how too much of it can weigh down your progress. We'll look at real examples of entrepreneurs who used credit strategically, as well as those who found themselves struggling under the weight of debt. Limiting reliance on credit is about building a business with stability and resilience — a foundation that doesn't crumble when faced with financial pressures. Let's dive into the principles of debt management and learn how to keep your business lean and agile.

Why Credit Can Be a Double-Edged Sword

Credit is like fuel. When used sparingly, it can help you accelerate your growth, purchase essential equipment, or hire new talent. But just as fuel can power a car or burn it to the ground, credit needs to be handled with caution. When you borrow too much or depend on credit to stay afloat, you're not just borrowing money; you're taking on risk and sacrificing some of your business's flexibility.

Take the case of WeWork, which initially soared on the promise of rapid growth and high-profile investments. The company took on significant debt to fuel its expansion, relying heavily on credit to secure leases, renovate spaces, and scale up faster than its revenue could support. When the market took a downturn and investor interest waned, WeWork found itself in a tight spot. Without the necessary cash flow to service its debt, the company's credit dependence exposed it to massive financial stress, leading to downsizing, restructuring, and a tarnished reputation.

WeWork's experience illustrates the danger of over-relying on borrowed money. In business, debt should be a tool, not a crutch. When credit becomes a necessity rather than a strategic choice, it limits your freedom to pivot, negotiate, or make long-term decisions.

When to Use Credit Wisely

Credit isn't inherently bad; in fact, it can be a powerful tool when used with a strategy in mind. The key is knowing when and how to use credit to your advantage rather than letting it control you. In general, credit works best when it's used for investments that directly contribute to your business's long-term value, such as:

Purchasing Essential Equipment: Credit can be valuable when acquiring equipment that directly drives revenue. For example, a photography business might use credit to purchase high-end cameras that enable it to offer premium services, or a restaurant might invest in kitchen upgrades to increase productivity and improve customer experience.

Real Estate and Property: Owning property or a dedicated workspace can be a sound investment. If buying real estate helps you cut down on long-term lease expenses and gives you a permanent location to grow from, taking on debt can be worth it. However, it's crucial to evaluate the risks and ensure your cash flow can handle the payments.

Scaling a Proven Business Model: If your business has a strong revenue stream and clear growth potential, credit can help scale operations. For example, if a retail store is highly profitable, using credit to open a second location may be a smart move. The key here is that you're building on an already successful model rather than using credit to fund uncertain ventures.

The key to using credit wisely is ensuring that the debt taken on has a direct path to generating income. By tying debt to revenue-generating assets or activities, you give yourself a chance to grow without risking financial stability.

The Risk of Using Credit for Day-to-Day Operations

One of the biggest mistakes businesses make is using credit to cover daily expenses — payroll, utilities, or rent. When credit becomes a lifeline for operational costs, it signals that the business isn't generating enough revenue to support itself. Using credit this way creates a cycle of dependency, where every month you're borrowing more just to stay afloat.

Take, for example, a small retail business that, during a slow season, decides to rely on a line of credit to cover rent and payroll. While this might seem like a short-term solution, it adds a financial burden that eats into profits when sales pick up again. Instead of reinvesting in inventory or marketing, the business is stuck paying off debt from the previous season. This kind of cycle traps businesses, forcing them to sacrifice growth for survival.

Credit for operational costs can lead to a debt trap, where you're constantly paying off yesterday's expenses instead of building for tomorrow. To avoid this, it's essential to build an emergency fund or a cash reserve, giving your business a cushion for slower periods without relying on credit.

The Freedom of a Debt-Free Business

Operating without debt offers a level of freedom and flexibility that credit-dependent businesses often lack. When you don't owe anyone, you have the power to make decisions based on your goals, not repayment schedules. A debt-free business can pivot quickly, respond to market changes, and seize opportunities without hesitation.

Patagonia, the outdoor clothing brand, exemplifies this freedom. The company has always emphasized sustainable growth, opting to reinvest profits rather than depend on credit for expansion. This approach has allowed Patagonia to stay true to its mission, prioritize quality, and avoid the pressure to chase profits at all costs. Without the burden of debt, Patagonia can focus on its values, maintain independence, and make strategic moves aligned with its vision.

Being debt-free isn't just about financial health; it's about independence. When your business isn't beholden to creditors or lenders, you're in control, allowing you to prioritize long-term growth over short-term demands.

Building an Emergency Fund

One of the best ways to avoid relying on credit for day-to-day expenses is by building an emergency fund. Just as individuals are advised to have savings for unexpected events, businesses benefit from having a financial buffer. An emergency fund allows you to cover short-term challenges, like unexpected expenses or a seasonal dip in sales, without needing to borrow.

Starbucks founder Howard Schultz prioritized building financial reserves in the early days of the company, even when it meant delaying expansion. Schultz understood that sustainable growth was more valuable than rapid scaling fueled by debt. This reserve helped Starbucks navigate economic downturns and market shifts, keeping the company stable even during challenging periods.

To start building an emergency fund, aim to save a percentage of your profits each month. Even setting aside 5-10% of revenue can create a safety net that keeps your business independent and resilient, able to weather storms without turning to credit.

Developing a Culture of Financial Discipline

Limiting reliance on credit isn't just a strategy; it's a mindset that can shape your entire company culture. When you prioritize financial discipline, your team understands the value of efficiency, careful spending, and resourcefulness. This culture of discipline not only protects your bottom line but also encourages innovation.

Southwest Airlines is known for its culture of financial discipline. Rather than relying on credit, the airline maximizes efficiency in everything from fuel usage to staff scheduling. By minimizing waste and avoiding unnecessary expenses, Southwest has built a reputation for profitability and stability, even in an industry that often struggles with debt. This focus on financial health has allowed Southwest to offer low fares while staying competitive.

Building a culture of financial discipline involves educating your team, setting clear budgets, and creating policies that prioritize careful spending. When everyone is aligned with the goal of financial independence, your business becomes more resilient, resourceful, and ready to grow sustainably.

Practical Tips for Minimizing Credit Reliance

Here are practical steps to limit reliance on credit and build a financially strong business:

Track Expenses Closely: Know where every dollar goes. Regularly monitor expenses and look for areas to cut costs, reinvesting savings into growth or an emergency fund.

Negotiate Payment Terms: With vendors, negotiate favorable payment terms to improve cash flow. A few extra weeks to pay an invoice can help you avoid borrowing to cover costs.

Prioritize Cash Flow Management: Cash flow is the lifeblood of any business. Focus on managing inflows and outflows to ensure you're generating enough to cover expenses without credit.

Focus on Revenue-Generating Activities: Invest in areas that directly contribute to revenue growth. This keeps your business profitable and reduces the need for outside funding.

Only Borrow for Strategic Growth: If you decide to use credit, make sure it's tied to a clear, revenue-driving initiative. Avoid debt for operational costs and ensure there's a return on investment.

Knowing When to Take a Calculated Risk

While limiting credit reliance is ideal, there may come a time when taking on debt is the right move. The key is to ensure that any borrowed funds are a calculated risk, tied directly to opportunities with measurable returns. For example, taking on credit to purchase equipment that will increase production or funding a marketing campaign for a product with proven demand can be strategic moves.

Jeff Bezos used a calculated risk approach when building Amazon's infrastructure. In the early days, Amazon took on debt to fund warehouses, allowing for faster shipping and improved customer experience. This strategic debt paid off as Amazon grew, transforming the company into the e-commerce giant it is today. Bezos didn't borrow recklessly; he borrowed with a clear vision, focused on future growth.

When you see an opportunity that aligns with your goals, evaluate the risks, potential rewards, and repayment timeline. A calculated risk should enhance your business's value, not create a burden that stifles flexibility.

Building Success Without the Weight of Debt

At its core, Biggie's commandment to "forget credit" reminds us to value independence. A business built on careful financial discipline, strategic investments, and self-sufficiency is positioned for long-term success. Limiting credit reliance allows you to control your growth pace, avoid unnecessary stress, and focus on what truly matters: creating value, serving your customers, and building something lasting.

As we move to the next chapter, remember that every financial decision you make shapes your future. In Chapter 7, we'll look at another essential commandment: Evaluate Family Involvement. Because while business is personal, it's also essential to separate family dynamics from professional needs. Turn the page, and let's explore how to balance family and business without losing focus.

Chapter 7: Evaluate Family Involvement

"Keep your family and business completely separated." — Notorious B.I.G.

Biggie's seventh commandment is one of his most straightforward: family and business should stay in their own lanes. The idea is simple, but when family and business mix, things can get complicated quickly. Blurring these lines can lead to tension, conflicts, and even resentment, making it hard to focus on what's best for the business. This doesn't mean that family can't support your goals or be a part of your journey; it simply means that boundaries are essential for both your business and your relationships.

In this chapter, we'll dive into the risks and rewards of family involvement, how to set boundaries when working with loved ones, and real-life examples of both successful and challenging family business dynamics. By the end of this chapter, you'll understand how to leverage family support while protecting your business and relationships, ensuring that each stays strong in its own right.

The Risks of Mixing Family and Business

Family involvement in a business can feel natural — you already have built-in trust, support, and often shared values. But with family, emotions run high, and stakes feel personal. When family dynamics enter a business setting, they can complicate decision-making, making it harder to separate what's best for the business from personal feelings. Here are a few common risks:

Conflicting Interests: Family members may prioritize their personal needs over business objectives. For example, a family member might push for decisions that benefit them directly rather than focusing on the company's broader goals.

Unclear Boundaries: When roles are unclear, family members can end up overstepping or assuming authority that wasn't granted to them. This lack of structure can lead to resentment and power struggles.

Difficulty in Addressing Performance Issues: When family members are involved, it can be challenging to address underperformance or behavior issues objectively. Critiquing a family member's work can lead to defensiveness or damage the relationship outside of work.

Entitlement and Expectations: Family members might feel entitled to special treatment, promotions, or job security regardless of performance. This can create tension among other employees and hinder merit-based growth.

Take, for example, the story of Forever 21, a retail empire that was originally a family business. The founders, Do Won and Jin Sook Chang, involved their children in the company's operations. While initially, this seemed like a natural fit, over time, differing visions and conflicting interests led to tension, ultimately contributing to the company's decline. The dynamics between family members, especially when personal goals clashed with business needs, impacted the company's stability, growth, and decision-making.

When Family Involvement Works

Not all family involvement is problematic. Some of the world's most successful businesses have a family at the core, with each member playing a clear, defined role. The key to successful family involvement is structure, communication, and alignment on shared goals. When everyone is clear on their roles, boundaries, and the business's vision, family involvement can strengthen a business rather than complicate it.

Consider the Mars family, which has built Mars Inc. — one of the world's largest privately held companies. Each family member who enters the business does so with a clear understanding of their role, and the company has a longstanding tradition of meritocracy, with a strong focus on aligning individual contributions with the company's goals. By structuring their involvement, the Mars family has kept business growth at the forefront while maintaining a healthy family dynamic.

Setting Boundaries: Defining Roles and Responsibilities

If you decide to involve family in your business, setting clear boundaries and defining roles from the outset is essential. Without structure, family dynamics can spill into the workplace, causing confusion and conflicts. Here's how to establish boundaries that protect both your relationships and the business:

Define Specific Roles: Each family member should have a specific job description that aligns with their skills and experience. Clarify what they're responsible for, who they report to, and what success looks like in their role.

Create a Chain of Command: Avoid ambiguity by establishing a clear hierarchy. Family members should understand that even though they're family, they're also part of a team and will follow the same rules and chain of command as everyone else.

Hold Regular Check-Ins: Schedule regular meetings to discuss progress, address any issues, and recalibrate goals. This formal structure keeps conversations about work separate from family gatherings, allowing you to address work matters in a business setting.

Separate Personal and Professional Relationships: Set boundaries around when work discussions are appropriate. For example, agree not to discuss business matters during family events, holidays, or dinners. This protects your personal relationships from business-related stress.

By creating structure and treating family members as you would any other team member, you reinforce the professionalism of your business and protect family relationships.

Transparency and Open Communication

Communication is always important in business, but when family is involved, transparency becomes even more essential. Family members need to feel valued and heard, but they also need to understand the company's goals, limitations, and expectations. Open communication ensures that everyone stays on the same page and that small misunderstandings don't grow into major issues.

The Rockefeller family, known for its legacy in business and philanthropy, exemplifies the importance of transparent communication. Each generation has been actively involved in maintaining the family's business and philanthropic efforts, but regular family meetings and open communication have kept their ventures cohesive. By promoting transparency, the Rockefellers have managed to pass down their values, ensuring that each member understands and respects the vision while contributing to its growth.

In your own business, set up regular check-ins, open forums, or even family retreats where business matters can be discussed openly. Creating these communication channels helps prevent assumptions and lets family members voice concerns in a constructive setting.

Managing Expectations and Entitlement

One of the trickiest aspects of family involvement is managing expectations. Family members may assume they'll have special privileges, job security, or a say in decisions simply because they're family. This sense of entitlement can lead to conflicts, especially with non-family employees who may feel that they're being treated unfairly.

To manage expectations, make it clear that family members are held to the same standards as other employees. Establish performance metrics, conduct regular reviews, and avoid giving family members special treatment. When everyone understands that merit drives advancement, you create a culture of fairness and accountability.

Consider the example of Ford Motor Company, which has maintained its family legacy while managing expectations. Members of the Ford family are not guaranteed high-level positions but must earn them through experience, performance, and contribution to the company's goals. By prioritizing merit over entitlement, Ford has kept the company competitive and respected, even with family members involved.

Knowing When It's Time to Step Back

Sometimes, the best decision for a business is to keep family involvement limited or non-existent. Not every family dynamic can adapt to the demands of a business environment, and that's okay. Recognizing when family involvement is hindering growth rather than supporting it is an essential skill for any entrepreneur.

The Gucci family provides a notable example of this. The luxury brand Gucci was originally a family-run business, but internal conflicts, power struggles, and a lack of alignment eventually led to family members leaving the company. While the decision was difficult, it ultimately allowed Gucci to thrive under new leadership and avoid the challenges that family dynamics had brought into the business.

Choosing to limit family involvement doesn't mean you're cutting off support; it means recognizing the need for professional distance. Sometimes, the healthiest choice is to let family be family, keeping business strictly business.

Practical Tips for Managing Family in Business

If you decide to involve family in your business, here are some practical steps to keep things running smoothly:

Create a Family Business Policy: Establish clear guidelines for how family members can join, what roles they're eligible for, and the process for promotions. Documenting these policies helps eliminate ambiguity and sets a professional tone.

Set Performance Standards: Just like any other employee, family members should be held to performance standards. Set measurable goals and conduct regular evaluations to ensure they're contributing effectively.

Develop an Exit Strategy: Plan for what will happen if a family member decides to leave the business or if their role needs to be redefined. Having a clear exit strategy prevents awkward conversations and ensures continuity.

Involve Non-Family Advisors: Bring in non-family board members, mentors, or advisors who can offer objective perspectives. These outsiders can provide balance and prevent family dynamics from clouding business decisions.

Define Compensation Clearly: Be transparent about salaries, bonuses, and other benefits for family members. Compensation should reflect the role and contribution, not familial status, to maintain a sense of fairness.

Creating a Legacy Without Family Ties

For some entrepreneurs, building a legacy means creating a business that isn't tied to family but stands strong on its own. This approach allows the business to be passed down to leaders based on merit and vision rather than familial relationships. Companies like IBM, known for their innovation and legacy, have succeeded by focusing on talent and leadership rather than family ties.

Building a business without family involvement can also allow you to create a legacy rooted in values and culture, making it attractive to a broader range of leaders. This approach frees the business from the complications of family dynamics, allowing it to adapt more fluidly to changes in the market.

Balancing Family Support and Independence

Family involvement doesn't have to mean direct participation in the business. Many entrepreneurs find that family can support their journey from a distance, offering encouragement, resources, and advice without getting involved in day-to-day operations. This balanced approach allows you to benefit from family support while maintaining independence in your business decisions.

A supportive family can act as a sounding board, helping you brainstorm, encouraging you through challenges, and offering perspective without directly influencing the business. By keeping family in a supportive but non-operational role, you protect your independence while still benefiting from their encouragement.

Building Success While Protecting Family Bonds

In the end, keeping family and business separate is about protecting what matters most. Family relationships are invaluable, and when they're healthy, they offer a sense of belonging and support that business can't replace. By respecting the boundary between family and business, you ensure that both can thrive independently.

Biggie's advice reminds us that our businesses and our families each have their place and keeping them separate is an act of respect. As we move to Chapter 8, we'll explore the next commandment: "Stay Ready for Competition." Because in business, the next challenge is always around the corner, and staying ready is the key to staying successful. Turn the page, and let's dive into how you can stay sharp, agile, and prepared for what's next.

Chapter 8: Stay Ready for Competition

"Don't keep your eyes on the prize, if you ain't ready to die for it." — *Notorious B.I.G.*

In business, staying ahead is all about being ready for the competition. Biggie's advice on keeping your eyes on the prize is a reminder that true focus and commitment aren't just about looking forward — they're about staying sharp, prepared to fight for what's yours. Competition is fierce, and in today's market, it can come from anywhere: a new startup with disruptive technology, an established company expanding into your field, or even an individual with a unique approach.

This chapter focuses on staying competitive, remaining adaptable, and cultivating the resilience needed to not only survive but thrive in a crowded market. Whether you're a small business in a growing industry or a large company in a mature market, staying ready for competition is about embracing change, innovating constantly, and understanding the landscape so that nothing catches you off guard.

Embracing a Competitive Mindset

To stay ready for competition, you need a competitive mindset. This doesn't mean viewing every business as a threat, but rather maintaining a constant awareness of the market and being willing to adapt quickly. A competitive mindset is fueled by curiosity, resilience, and a commitment to continuous improvement.

Consider Jeff Bezos, founder of Amazon. Bezos has always had a competitive mindset, famously saying, "Your margin is my opportunity." Instead of fearing competitors, Bezos views competition as a motivator to push Amazon's capabilities further, consistently challenging his teams to innovate, improve efficiencies, and deliver value. Bezos's commitment to outpacing competitors has positioned Amazon as a dominant player across industries, from e-commerce to cloud computing.

A competitive mindset doesn't just keep you focused; it fuels growth. By embracing competition as an opportunity to sharpen your edge, you become more resilient, adaptable, and better equipped to handle challenges.

Knowing Your Competitors Inside and Out

One of the most effective ways to stay ready for competition is to know who your competitors are, what they're doing, and where their strengths and weaknesses lie. This isn't just about tracking their latest products or services; it's about understanding their strategies, values, and target audiences. By knowing your competitors deeply, you gain insights that can help you differentiate yourself and find gaps in the market.

Southwest Airlines, for example, has long been known for its customer-friendly approach to air travel. In the highly competitive airline industry, Southwest didn't just compete on price; it studied its competitors to identify where it could provide a unique value — friendly service, no baggage fees, and a simplified fare structure. By understanding the weaknesses in traditional airline models, Southwest carved out a niche that set it apart, creating loyal customers and sustained growth.

To stay competitive, analyze your competitors' strengths, weaknesses, and strategies. Identify where they excel and where they fall short. Use this information not to copy, but to differentiate your own offerings, aligning your strengths with market needs.

Adapting Quickly: The Key to Staying Ahead

Competition changes rapidly, and businesses that can't adapt are often left behind. Staying competitive requires flexibility — a willingness to pivot, change course, and adopt new technologies or strategies as needed. Adapting doesn't mean abandoning your vision; it means finding new ways to reach it when the environment shifts.

Take Netflix as an example. Originally a DVD rental company, Netflix saw the potential of streaming technology early on and made the pivot before many of its competitors had even considered it. By transitioning to a streaming model and later investing in original content, Netflix stayed ahead of Blockbuster and other traditional media companies that were slower to adapt. Netflix's ability to stay flexible and respond to market changes has kept it relevant and competitive, even as the entertainment industry undergoes constant disruption.

To stay adaptable, foster a culture of experimentation within your business. Encourage your team to propose new ideas, test different approaches, and embrace change. Flexibility keeps you light on your feet, ready to respond when opportunities or challenges arise.

Innovating for Longevity

In a competitive market, innovation is essential for longevity. It's not enough to simply react to what your competitors are doing; you need to lead with fresh ideas, products, or services that capture customer interest and set new standards. True innovation isn't about reinventing the wheel; it's about finding unique ways to solve problems and create value that keeps customers coming back.

Apple's approach to innovation has kept it at the forefront of the tech industry for decades. The company didn't invent the smartphone, but it redefined what a smartphone could be with the launch of the iPhone. By focusing on design, user experience, and an ecosystem that integrates devices seamlessly, Apple created a product that competitors struggled to match. Apple's dedication to innovation — not just in products but in customer experience — has set it apart and given it a loyal following.

In your business, look for areas where you can innovate. Whether it's in product design, customer service, or user experience, find ways to add unique value that competitors aren't offering. Innovation sets you apart, makes your brand memorable, and ensures that customers have a reason to choose you over others.

Leveraging Data for Competitive Advantage

In today's market, data is a powerful tool that can give you insights into customer behavior, market trends, and competitor activity. By leveraging data, you can make informed decisions, anticipate changes, and stay one step ahead of competitors who may still be guessing. The ability to analyze and act on data is no longer optional — it's essential.

Uber's rise to dominance in the ride-sharing industry is a prime example of data-driven strategy. By tracking user data, analyzing ride patterns, and predicting demand, Uber optimized its pricing, improved wait times, and expanded strategically into new cities. Uber didn't just rely on intuition; it used data to refine its service, expand efficiently, and respond to customer needs faster than its competitors.

If you want to stay competitive, invest in data collection and analysis. Track customer preferences, monitor market trends, and regularly assess performance metrics. Data-driven insights help you make precise adjustments to your strategy, ensuring you stay responsive and relevant.

Building a Team Ready to Compete

A competitive business needs a competitive team. Your people are your most valuable asset, and their skills, dedication, and creativity play a significant role in staying ahead. Building a team that's ready to compete means hiring individuals who are not only talented but also resilient, adaptable, and committed to continuous growth.

Consider Google's hiring practices. Google is known for recruiting employees who not only have technical skills but also bring innovation, curiosity, and a passion for solving problems. The company emphasizes a growth mindset, encouraging employees to push boundaries, experiment, and think creatively. This approach has helped Google maintain its competitive edge, as employees are constantly striving to improve and innovate.

To build a competitive team, focus on recruiting individuals who align with your vision and are driven to excel. Invest in their growth through training, mentorship, and opportunities for skill development. A team that's prepared to face challenges head-on can be a decisive advantage in a competitive market.

Balancing Competition with Collaboration

While competition drives innovation and keeps you sharp, collaboration can also be a powerful tool for growth. In certain situations, forming alliances with competitors or other businesses can open doors to new markets, improve efficiencies, and enhance customer value. Collaboration doesn't mean you're abandoning your competitive edge; it means you're finding strategic ways to strengthen it.

Starbucks and PepsiCo, for example, collaborated to create the highly successful line of bottled Frappuccino drinks. While Starbucks could have competed in the bottled beverage market alone, partnering with PepsiCo allowed it to leverage Pepsi's distribution network and resources. The result was a win-win: Starbucks gained a new revenue stream, and Pepsi expanded its product portfolio.

In your own industry, consider where collaboration might complement your competitive efforts. Whether through partnerships, joint ventures, or collaborations on special projects, strategic alliances can give you access to resources, expertise, or markets that might be difficult to achieve alone.

Resilience: The Ultimate Competitive Advantage

Staying ready for competition isn't just about strategy and skill; it's about resilience. The business landscape is unpredictable, and even the best plans can be thrown off course by unexpected challenges. Building resilience means being prepared to adapt, recover, and keep moving forward, no matter what obstacles arise.

Nike's resilience during the 2008 financial crisis is a testament to this. When consumer spending dropped, Nike didn't just cut costs and wait for recovery; it invested in product innovation and focused on building customer loyalty. By doubling down on its brand, Nike emerged from the recession stronger, with a more loyal customer base and a greater market share.

Resilience is built through preparation, flexibility, and a willingness to learn from setbacks. Foster a resilient culture within your business by encouraging a growth mindset, embracing change, and viewing challenges as opportunities to improve. With resilience, you're not just prepared for competition — you're equipped to outlast it.

Practical Steps to Stay Competitive

To keep your business competitive, here are actionable steps you can take:

Conduct Regular Competitor Analysis: Continuously monitor competitors' offerings, pricing, and customer feedback. Use this information to adjust your strategy and identify areas where you can stand out.

Invest in Innovation: Set aside resources for research and development. Encourage your team to experiment, propose new ideas, and explore potential improvements in products or services.

Build a Data-Driven Culture: Use data to make informed decisions. Regularly review performance metrics, customer feedback, and market trends to stay responsive.

Develop a Growth Mindset: Foster a culture where challenges are viewed as opportunities to learn. Encourage your team to embrace change, adapt, and continuously improve.

Plan for Contingencies: Prepare for disruptions by creating backup plans. Having contingency strategies allows you to respond quickly when the unexpected happens.

Winning the Long Game

At the end of the day, competition is inevitable, but it's also what drives us to be better. Staying ready for competition means more than just keeping an eye on rivals; it means actively preparing yourself and your business to meet challenges head-on. By cultivating a competitive mindset, innovating constantly, and building resilience, you're not just surviving — you're setting yourself up to win the long game.

Biggie's commandment is a reminder that business, like life, requires commitment and readiness. Keep your eyes on the prize, stay prepared to defend what you've built, and remember that competition is a force that can propel you forward when you're ready to face it. In Chapter 9, we'll explore the next commandment: Maintain Your Reputation. Because in business, your name is everything, and protecting it is just as important as staying competitive. Turn the page, and let's talk about safeguarding the legacy you're building.

Chapter 9: Maintain Your Reputation

"If you ain't got the clientele, say hell no." — Notorious B.I.G.

Biggie's ninth commandment reminds us that reputation is everything. In his world, having a strong reputation wasn't just about having clients; it was about maintaining credibility, consistency, and respect. In business, reputation works the same way. Your reputation is your brand, your calling card, and the foundation of trust between you and your clients, customers, and partners. Building a solid reputation is hard work but losing it can happen in an instant. Maintaining that respect means keeping promises, delivering value, and managing relationships with care.

This chapter is about understanding the impact of reputation on long-term success, practical strategies to build and protect it, and examples of companies that have safeguarded their names. We'll explore how to consistently show up for clients, handle mistakes with integrity, and keep your brand strong so that people know they can count on you.

Why Reputation Is Your Most Valuable Asset

In a marketplace crowded with options, reputation is often what sets businesses apart. A strong reputation means people trust you to deliver, even if they've never worked with you before. When clients know that you're reliable, transparent, and focused on quality, they're more likely to choose you over a competitor — and to return when they need your services again. But a tarnished reputation can be costly, pushing people away and forcing you to work twice as hard to regain lost trust.

Take Toyota, for example. In 2010, the company faced a major recall crisis when millions of vehicles were found to have unintended acceleration issues. The situation could have been catastrophic for Toyota's reputation as a reliable car manufacturer. However, Toyota took swift action, addressing the issue head-on, communicating transparently with customers, and implementing rigorous quality control processes. While the recall affected their short-term sales, Toyota's prompt, responsible response helped restore its reputation. Today, it remains one of the world's leading automakers.

In business, your reputation acts as a buffer during crises. When people know they can trust you, they're more likely to stick with you through challenging times. A strong reputation is a competitive advantage that keeps customers loyal, builds resilience, and allows you to navigate tough moments with grace.

Consistency: Showing Up, Every Time

Consistency is at the heart of a strong reputation. It's not enough to deliver excellence once; clients and customers need to know they can rely on you every time. Consistency means showing up with the same quality, focus, and integrity, no matter the situation. When you're consistent, you're building trust one interaction at a time, creating a reputation that people remember.

Look at Coca-Cola. For over a century, Coca-Cola has delivered a product that tastes the same whether you're in Atlanta, Tokyo, or Cape Town. This consistency has built trust with consumers around the world, creating a brand that's instantly recognizable. Coca-Cola's commitment to quality and consistency has allowed it to dominate the soft drink market and create a reputation that's lasted generations.

In your own business, focus on building consistency across all touchpoints — from customer service to product quality to the way you communicate. When clients know they can expect the same high standards every time, you're creating a brand they'll return to again and again.

Managing Mistakes with Integrity

In business, mistakes are inevitable. But how you handle them can make or break your reputation. Owning up to errors, addressing them transparently, and taking steps to prevent future issues shows clients that you're committed to integrity. When people see that you're willing to take responsibility, they're more likely to forgive and even respect you for your honesty.

Consider Johnson & Johnson's response to the 1982 Tylenol crisis. After discovering that several bottles of Tylenol had been tampered with, resulting in deaths, Johnson & Johnson issued a nationwide recall, even though it wasn't legally required to do so. The company communicated openly with the public and developed tamper-proof packaging to restore consumer confidence. Johnson & Johnson's swift and transparent response didn't just save its reputation; it reinforced the company's commitment to customer safety and trust.

Mistakes don't have to ruin your reputation. In fact, they can be opportunities to demonstrate your values and reinforce your commitment to customers. By managing mistakes with integrity, you show people that your business stands for more than profit; it stands for accountability.

Delivering Value: The Foundation of Loyalty

A strong reputation is built on delivering real value to your clients or customers. Value isn't just about price; it's about the quality, experience, and reliability you offer. When people feel they're getting more than what they paid for, they become loyal, referring you to others and returning when they need your services again.

Apple has mastered the art of delivering value. Its products are often more expensive than competitors, but customers are willing to pay because they know they're getting high-quality design, innovation, and customer service. Apple has created a reputation for excellence that keeps people coming back, even when cheaper options are available. By consistently delivering value, Apple has built a brand that people trust and admire.

To build a reputation for delivering value, focus on understanding your customers' needs and exceeding their expectations. Go beyond the basics, offering personalized support, reliable products, and a seamless experience that shows clients you're invested in their satisfaction.

Building Relationships with Clients and Customers

Your reputation isn't just about the product or service you offer; it's about the relationships you build with your clients and customers. When you take the time to get to know them, understand their needs, and offer personalized support, you're creating connections that go beyond transactions. These relationships create loyal customers who see you as more than just a service provider; they see you as a partner in their success.

Take Zappos, the online shoe retailer, as an example. Zappos built its reputation on exceptional customer service, going above and beyond to make customers feel valued. From free shipping to an incredibly generous return policy, Zappos shows customers that it cares about their experience. Zappos's commitment to building relationships has earned it a reputation as one of the most customer-centric brands in retail.

In your own business, focus on building genuine connections with your clients. Listen to their needs, follow up regularly, and make an effort to show appreciation. When clients feel valued, they're more likely to spread the word, bringing in new business and strengthening your reputation.

Staying Transparent: The Key to Trust

Transparency is a cornerstone of trust, especially in today's world where consumers are more informed and discerning than ever. Being upfront about your processes, pricing, and policies helps clients feel confident in their decision to work with you. Transparency isn't just a nice-to-have; it's a necessity for building a strong, lasting reputation.

Patagonia, the outdoor apparel company, has built its reputation on transparency, particularly when it comes to sustainability. Patagonia openly shares information about its supply chain, environmental impact, and ethical sourcing practices. This transparency has earned it the trust and respect of consumers who prioritize sustainability, helping Patagonia stand out in a competitive market.

Incorporate transparency into your business practices by being open about what clients can expect, from turnaround times to pricing. If there's an issue, communicate it honestly rather than trying to cover it up. When people see that you're transparent, they're more likely to trust you and view your business as one with integrity.

Protecting Your Brand in the Digital Age

In today's digital world, reputation management is more important than ever. One negative review, a single misstep on social media, or a complaint that goes viral can damage your reputation in an instant. To protect your brand, it's essential to monitor your online presence, respond to feedback promptly, and handle criticism professionally.

Consider the example of Starbucks. The company has had its share of social media challenges, facing backlash over issues related to service, pricing, and social stances. However, Starbucks has shown a willingness to engage with its audience, respond to criticism, and, when necessary, adjust its policies. This approach has helped Starbucks maintain a strong reputation, even when facing negative publicity.

To protect your brand, make online reputation management a priority. Monitor reviews, respond to comments on social media, and address complaints promptly. By showing clients that you're attentive and willing to listen, you reinforce the positive aspects of your reputation and build a community that supports your brand.

Practical Tips for Building and Maintaining Your Reputation

Building a strong reputation is an ongoing process that requires consistency, integrity, and focus. Here are some practical tips to help you maintain your reputation:

Keep Promises: Don't overpromise and underdeliver. Set realistic expectations, and make sure you follow through on your commitments. Reliability builds trust.

Ask for Feedback: Regularly ask clients for feedback to show that you're committed to improving. Use their insights to make meaningful changes and reinforce your dedication to quality.

Invest in Quality: Focus on delivering high-quality products or services that meet your customers' needs. Quality is the foundation of a solid reputation.

Celebrate Successes Publicly: Don't be afraid to share client success stories, testimonials, or case studies. This showcases your impact and reinforces your reputation for delivering results.

Handle Criticism Gracefully: Negative feedback is inevitable, but responding calmly and professionally shows that you care about improvement. Don't ignore criticism; use it as a tool to strengthen your business.

Building a Legacy of Trust

At the end of the day, reputation is about trust. It's about showing clients, customers, and partners that you're someone they can rely on, someone who will deliver value and uphold integrity in every interaction. A strong reputation doesn't just bring in business; it creates a legacy that lasts, allowing your business to grow on the foundation of trust and respect.

Biggie's advice to "keep the clientele" speaks to this commitment. If people don't trust you, they won't stick around. By focusing on quality, consistency, transparency, and customer relationships, you're building something bigger than sales — you're building loyalty, respect, and a lasting impact.

In Chapter 10, we'll explore Biggie's final commandment: Keep Hustling. Because once you've built a reputation, the journey doesn't end; it's only the beginning of the work needed to protect, grow, and evolve your legacy. Turn the page, and let's dive into the mindset that keeps winners in the game long after they've hit their first success.

Chapter 10: Keep Hustling

"Ten crack commandments, can't tell me nothin'." — Notorious B.I.G.

Biggie's final commandment is the ultimate truth for any entrepreneur, hustler, or business leader. It's about resilience, persistence, and never letting up. Hustling isn't just a phase; it's a mindset. When you've reached a certain level, it's easy to get comfortable or start coasting. But the real champions know that there's always another level to reach, a new challenge to face, and an opportunity to push the boundaries. In business, there's no "finish line" — just new heights waiting to be conquered.

This chapter is about the drive that fuels long-term success. It's about staying hungry, evolving with the times, and keeping that fire alive long after the initial success fades. We'll look at how to keep hustling when things get tough, why embracing the grind is essential, and how to continue growing and reinventing yourself to stay relevant. The final commandment is a reminder that no matter how far you've come, the journey is far from over.

The Hustler's Mindset: Always Moving Forward

Hustling isn't just about putting in long hours or chasing after every opportunity. True hustling is about having a relentless drive to grow, learn, and improve, no matter where you are in your career. The hustler's mindset is one that constantly seeks progress, refusing to settle for "good enough." It's about staying curious, ambitious, and willing to push through challenges.

Consider the story of Sara Blakely, the founder of Spanx. When she started, she faced rejection after rejection as she tried to get her product into stores. But Blakely kept hustling, determined to make her vision a reality. Her persistence paid off, turning Spanx into a billion-dollar brand. Even after reaching immense success, Blakely continued to innovate and explore new ideas, never becoming complacent.

A hustler's mindset means staying humble and always looking for ways to improve. It's about not letting your past wins define your future and recognizing that every day is a chance to build something new, make a difference, and elevate your work. When you keep moving forward, you stay ahead of the game, pushing past limits others set for themselves.

Embracing the Grind: Hard Work as a Habit

There's a romanticized idea of overnight success, but real hustlers know that true success is built on hard work, often done quietly and over time. Embracing the grind means recognizing that there will be late nights, early mornings, setbacks, and sacrifices. But each step in the journey adds to your experience and resilience.

Think of Dwayne "The Rock" Johnson, a figure synonymous with hard work. Starting as a wrestler and pivoting to acting, Johnson has built an empire. His success didn't happen by accident — it was a product of countless hours of preparation, practice, and a relentless work ethic. The Rock is known for his "clanging and banging" workout sessions, up before dawn, putting in the work when no one's watching. His grind is a habit, not a one-time push, and it's this consistency that's built his career.

When you embrace the grind, hard work becomes a habit, something you do instinctively. You stop waiting for motivation and start relying on discipline. Every step you take brings you closer to your goals, and the progress compounds, turning effort into results over time.

Reinventing Yourself: Staying Relevant

In business, what worked yesterday might not work tomorrow. Staying relevant means continuously evolving, reinventing yourself, and adapting to new market needs. The most successful entrepreneurs know that complacency is the enemy of growth. They keep learning, pivoting, and finding new ways to add value.

Take Madonna, an artist known for reinventing herself time and again. For decades, she's stayed relevant not just through her music, but by adapting her image, sound, and style to match the times. Madonna's willingness to embrace change has kept her at the forefront of the music industry, connecting with new generations of fans while remaining true to her core identity.

In your business, reinvention might mean learning new skills, adopting new technology, or expanding into different markets. Staying relevant isn't about changing who you are; it's about evolving in a way that allows you to keep growing and contributing meaningfully. By embracing change, you keep yourself open to new possibilities and remain a force to be reckoned with.

Resilience: Bouncing Back from Setbacks

The hustle is full of highs and lows. No matter how successful you are, setbacks are inevitable, and the ability to bounce back is what separates those who continue to grow from those who give up. Resilience is about embracing failure as part of the journey and using it as a tool for growth.

Consider the story of Oprah Winfrey. Early in her career, Oprah faced significant obstacles, including being told she was "unfit for television." Instead of letting rejection stop her, Oprah kept pushing forward, eventually creating a media empire. Her resilience in the face of setbacks has inspired millions, and it's what's allowed her to make a lasting impact across industries.

Building resilience starts with a mindset that sees challenges as opportunities. It's about understanding that failure is not the end, but a stepping stone toward success. When you cultivate resilience, you become stronger with each setback, and the hustle becomes a journey of learning, growth, and transformation.

The Power of Adaptability

In today's fast-paced world, adaptability is one of the most important qualities you can have. The business landscape is constantly changing, with new technologies, trends, and market demands emerging all the time. Staying adaptable means being open to learning, trying new approaches, and pivoting when necessary.

Netflix is a prime example of adaptability. The company started as a DVD rental service, but as streaming technology evolved, Netflix pivoted its business model. This adaptability not only saved Netflix but also allowed it to lead the streaming revolution, becoming one of the most influential entertainment companies in the world. Netflix's willingness to adapt and explore new business models has kept it relevant and competitive in an industry known for rapid change.

To stay adaptable, approach each day as a learning opportunity. Embrace change rather than resisting it and be willing to question old methods if new solutions are better. Adaptability isn't about losing focus; it's about staying flexible enough to capitalize on new opportunities.

Staying Hungry: Never Settling

Even after achieving success, staying hungry is essential. True hustlers understand that success is never final. They keep pushing, exploring, and innovating, knowing that there's always room for improvement. Staying hungry means refusing to coast, even when things are going well, and continuing to strive for more.

Elon Musk exemplifies the concept of staying hungry. Despite building successful companies like PayPal, Tesla, and SpaceX, Musk is constantly pushing himself to explore new frontiers, from space exploration to renewable energy. Musk's hunger for progress and innovation keeps him moving forward, unafraid to tackle new challenges and disrupt industries.

Staying hungry doesn't mean you're never satisfied; it means you recognize that growth is a lifelong journey. When you're driven by curiosity and ambition, you never reach a point where you feel you've "made it." You keep aiming higher, challenging yourself to reach new heights and leave a legacy that's meaningful.

Practical Tips for Keeping the Hustle Alive

Keeping the hustle alive requires intention and commitment. Here are practical ways to maintain your drive, even when success starts to come your way:

Set New Goals Regularly: After achieving one goal, set another. New goals keep you focused, challenge you to grow, and prevent you from becoming complacent.

Stay Curious: Continue learning by reading, attending workshops, and surrounding yourself with people who inspire you. Curiosity fuels growth and keeps your perspective fresh.

Celebrate Small Wins: Recognizing your progress keeps you motivated. Celebrate the small victories along the way to remind yourself that each step is part of the journey.

Network with Other Hustlers: Surround yourself with people who share your drive and ambition. Networking with others who are passionate about growth keeps you inspired and focused.

Reflect on Your Purpose: Regularly revisit why you started. Connecting with your purpose reinforces your commitment and keeps you grounded when challenges arise.

The Legacy of Hustling: Building Something That Lasts

At the heart of the hustle is the desire to create something lasting — a legacy that lives beyond you. For many, hustling is about more than just financial success; it's about making a difference, creating value, and leaving an impact. When you're hustling with purpose, every step you take is part of a larger story.

Jay-Z, the rapper turned entrepreneur, is a prime example of someone who's built a legacy through relentless hustle. Starting from humble beginnings, Jay-Z used his talent, ambition, and business savvy to create a career that spans music, fashion, sports, and more. His journey wasn't just about personal success; it was about creating opportunities for others, inspiring a generation, and proving that greatness is within reach if you're willing to hustle for it.

Building a legacy means keeping your eyes on the big picture. It's about doing work that matters, creating value that lasts, and inspiring others along the way. When your hustle is driven by purpose, you're building something that endures, something that makes a lasting difference.

Hustling Isn't Just About Work — It's About Growth

In the end, hustling is a journey of growth. It's not just about achieving goals but about becoming a better version of yourself, pushing past limits, and constantly evolving. Every challenge, every victory, and every setback shapes you, building resilience, discipline, and wisdom along the way. The hustle is as much about who you become as it is about what you achieve.

Biggie's final commandment reminds us that there's always more to learn, more to build, and more to achieve. Keep hustling, stay curious, and never settle. In business and in life, the hustle is a journey that doesn't end — it's a way of life that keeps you moving forward, constantly reaching for new heights.

As we close this book, remember that these ten commandments aren't just rules: they're a blueprint for building a career, a legacy, and a life that's rich in meaning. Hustling isn't just a phase; it's the foundation of lasting success. Embrace the journey, stay true to yourself, and keep pushing. The hustle continues.

Final Chapter: Living by the Code

"It's rules to this shit, I wrote me a manual." — *Notorious B.I.G.*

Here we are — the final chapter. We've walked through each of Biggie's commandments and applied them to the business world. We've explored the lessons, mindsets, and principles that build a foundation for lasting success. But these "rules" aren't just a set of guidelines. They're a code, a philosophy to live by. It's about more than building a successful business or climbing a career ladder. It's about embracing a way of life that keeps you grounded, hungry, and committed to growth, no matter what stage you're at.

Living by this code means holding yourself to a standard. It means pushing through the grind, making sacrifices, and valuing integrity, trust, and resilience. It's not about shortcuts or easy wins; it's about putting in the work, respecting the process, and knowing that success is built on a strong foundation. This final chapter is about making these lessons part of who you are, using them to guide your journey, and creating a legacy that's truly yours.

The Journey: More Than Just Success

Success in business, as in life, is rarely straightforward. It's a journey filled with twists, setbacks, and surprises. The code you live by isn't just about reaching a destination; it's about navigating the path with purpose, discipline, and self-respect. Biggie's commandments are reminders that each step you take, every decision you make, adds up to something much bigger.

Consider the life of Kobe Bryant, whose "Mamba Mentality" became a philosophy for excellence in and outside of basketball. For Kobe, success wasn't just about winning games; it was about the relentless pursuit of growth, the drive to master every detail, and the refusal to settle. Even after he retired from basketball, Kobe brought the same level of focus and dedication to new ventures in film, storytelling, and business. His legacy reminds us that the journey isn't about fame or fortune; it's about personal evolution.

When you approach success as a journey, you stay open to learning, willing to adapt, and committed to self-improvement. Living by this code keeps you grounded and focused, even when the path isn't clear. It's not about where you end up; it's about the impact you make along the way.

The Legacy of Hustle

Your work isn't just a means to an end; it's a testament to who you are. The hustle, the grind, the setbacks — these are all parts of a legacy you're building. When people remember you, they'll remember your consistency, your integrity, and the way you showed up when things got tough. Your reputation isn't built overnight, and it isn't destroyed by a single setback. It's a reflection of the commitment you bring every day.

Think of Maya Angelou, a writer, poet, and activist who used her voice to inspire and uplift generations. Angelou's legacy wasn't just her work; it was her resilience, her wisdom, and her relentless commitment to truth. She lived by a code of honesty, courage, and integrity, building a legacy that continues to inspire. Her life reminds us that true success is measured by the lives we touch and the impact we leave behind.

By living by the code, you're building a legacy that extends beyond profits or achievements. You're creating a lasting impact — something that speaks to who you are, what you believe, and the value you bring to the world.

Staying Grounded and Humble

The hustle can take you far, but staying grounded is what keeps you connected to your purpose. Humility is a key ingredient to growth; it reminds you that there's always more to learn and that success doesn't mean you stop working. Staying grounded means respecting the journey, appreciating the people who support you, and remaining true to your values.

Take LeBron James, an athlete who has remained humble despite his immense success. LeBron uses his platform not just for personal gain but to support his community, empower young people, and advocate for social justice. Despite his accomplishments, LeBron stays grounded, recognizing that his success is an opportunity to make a difference.

Staying humble doesn't mean you downplay your achievements; it means you recognize that success is a privilege, not a right. It's a mindset that values gratitude over entitlement, relationships over ego, and learning over complacency.

The Art of Giving Back

Success means little if it doesn't serve others. Giving back is a core part of the code, a reminder that true fulfillment comes from contributing to something bigger than yourself. When you give back — whether through mentorship, community support, or charitable efforts — you create a ripple effect that amplifies your impact.

Consider the legacy of Muhammad Ali. Known for his achievements in boxing, Ali also used his fame to champion causes that mattered to him. He fought for social justice, spoke out against oppression, and supported humanitarian efforts around the world. Ali's legacy extends far beyond sports; it's a testament to his commitment to uplift others and inspire change.

Giving back doesn't just enhance your legacy; it keeps you connected to your purpose. It reminds you that success is a shared journey and that each of us has the power to uplift, inspire, and make a difference. By contributing to the world around you, you're building a legacy that resonates long after you're gone.

Staying Hungry, Staying Focused

Living by the code means keeping that fire alive, that hunger to grow, learn, and push forward. No matter how far you've come, staying hungry ensures that you never lose sight of what's possible. It's about having the courage to dream big, the discipline to work for it, and the resilience to keep going, even when things get tough.

Look at Rihanna, an artist who didn't stop with music but expanded her reach into fashion, beauty, and business. Rihanna's ambition led her to create Fenty Beauty, a brand that challenged industry norms by promoting inclusivity and diversity. Her drive to keep innovating, to stay relevant, and to push boundaries has made her a powerhouse in multiple industries.

Staying hungry doesn't mean chasing fame or fortune; it means remaining committed to growth. It's a mindset that embraces change, challenges limits, and celebrates each step forward. When you stay focused on the hustle, you're constantly working toward your best self, no matter how much success you've already achieved.

Living by the Code: A Way of Life

In the end, Biggie's commandments aren't just about business; they're about a way of life. They're a reminder that success isn't just about what you do but how you do it. It's about keeping your integrity, respecting the journey, and building a legacy that reflects who you are. Living by the code means embracing the hustle as a lifelong journey, one that values hard work, resilience, and purpose.

The code isn't a set of rules; it's a mindset that guides every decision, every relationship, and every goal. It's a commitment to growth, integrity, and impact, no matter where life takes you. And it's a promise to yourself that you'll stay true to who you are, keep pushing forward, and never stop building a life and career that you're proud of.

The Journey Continues

As you close this book, remember that the journey is just beginning. The lessons, principles, and values in these pages are tools for building something real, something lasting. Embrace the hustle, live by the code, and stay committed to the journey. Success isn't a destination; it's a way of life, a constant pursuit of growth, purpose, and impact.

So, keep hustling. Stay focused, stay grounded, and remember that each step you take is part of a legacy that's uniquely yours. You're not just building a business; you're building a life, a story, a legacy that will inspire those who come after you. Live by the code, and let it guide you to heights you never imagined.

www.ingramcontent.com/pod-product-compliance
Lightning Source LLC
Chambersburg PA
CBHW071055240526

45469CB00006BD/2300